# Highlife Music in West Africa
*Down memory lane...*

# Highlife Music in West Africa
## *Down memory lane...*

Professor Sonny Oti
*Formerly of the Department of Theatre Arts
University of Jos, Jos,
Nigeria*

**Malthouse Press Limited**
Lagos, Benin, Ibadan, Jos, Port-Harcourt, Zaria

**Malthouse Press Limited**
41 Onitana Street, Off Stadium Hotel Road,
Surulere, Lagos, Lagos State
E-mail: malthouse_press@yahoo.com
malthouselagos@gmail.com
Tel: +234 (01) -773 53 44; 0802 600 3203

All rights reserved. No part of this publication may be reproduced, transmitted, transcribed, stored in a retrieval system or translated into any language or computer language, in any form or by any means, electronic, mechanical, magnetic, chemical, thermal, manual or otherwise, without the prior consent in writing of Malthouse Press Limited, Lagos, Nigeria.

This book is sold subject to the condition that it shall not by way of trade, or otherwise, be lent, re-sold, hired out, or otherwise circulated without the publisher's prior consent in writing, in any form of binding or cover other than in which it is published and without a similar condition, including this condition, being imposed on the subsequent purchaser.

© Sonny Oti 2009
First Published 2009
ISBN 978-978-8422-08-2

*Distributors:*

African Books Collective
Oxford, United Kingdom
Email: abc@africanbookscollective.com
Website: http://www.africanbookscollective.com

# Dedication

## I

For my daughter Ndidi Nnennaya Oti: (of Blessed Memory) a beloved child of God now in Abraham's bossom.

## II

for PMAN:
Performing Musicians
Association of Nigeria.

------the copyright law is the evidence-----

# Acknowledgements

There is no way a book can be made without the support and goodwill from persons the author will remember many years after the project. Sometimes, the author is not ungrateful to some contributors, but falls prey to memory slip in crediting all who helped one way or other towards the building of the book. To such persons, I give my unreserved apology.

For field work, my credits go to these young university graduates and undergraduates: Meg Etim, Amayo Philips, Badmus Onifade, Ekaete Inyang, Victor Anoliefo and others.

Charles Kalu assisted me in tidying up the manuscript after it was formally assessed publishable.

Benedette Nwiyi transcribed all the interview tapes, picked up relevant magazines, dailies, etc. for me and was always alert to any useful information while working for her JAMB and WAEC. John Igwe, working for the Ministry of Works at Abakaliki, typed the first draft of the manuscript. He is experienced, painstaking and meticulous. Their services were continuous for one full year, 1984/85. I am indebted to them. Credit also goes to Chidiebere Igwe for transcribing Mike Ejeagha's tape from Igbo to English.

To Radio Nigeria, Enugu, my profound gratitude goes; to Mukosolu Nwobodo (Mrs) Controller of presentations; Christie Okonkwo (Mrs) - Principal Librarian and Peter Oriri, both of the Gramophone Library, as well as my sister, Mrs Mary Onucha of FRCN, Enugu, for contacts.

Of course, Chris Ijomah, Deputy Director of Programmes, of ABSTV, Enugu and his family, were by my side throughout. Clara Effiong, a graduate of my Department, was outstanding as a field assistant in making this book possible. So also was Chima Umeh, an undergraduate of my department, who covered an immense area patiently, interviewing all the musicians except Victor Uwaifo, Bala Miller, Bongos Ikwue, Inyang Henshaw, Etubom Rex Williams, and E. C. Arinze.

The assistance from Dr. Abu Abarry-Ali and Dr. Emmanuel O.

Quacco, both Ghanaian scholars, lecturing at the University of Jos, was significant in providing an essay which I included in the chapter on Ghana repertory.

Chief Stephen Osita Osadebe the highlife superstar, popularly known as belonging to the old and the new in highlife, deserves profound gratitude for offering me sixteen of his LP albums, including his 1984/85 top-of-the-chart, "Osondi Owendi." He also accommodated and entertained me lavishly during an interview contact which kept me two days as his guest. He also gave me generous cash to take care of my transport. Bongos Ikwue was very hospitable at his Tin-Can Island home at Lagos in 1980, where I had a long day with him. He did also give me a good number of his albums to contribute to the making of this book. Mike Ejeagba was excited at my initiative for a book of this nature. He gave moral inspiration and an album.

Mr. Boniface Leva granted me the use of his field work tape recorder. It was of immense help. Mr. Francis Ngwaba, Head of English Department at the University of Jos, shared ideas with me; and I am grateful. Mr. Chris Akwarandu, a former student of our department, contributed in putting the pages together.

My gratitude to Mr. Gab Okwudire, an executive of The Registry at the University of Jos, without whom an excellent typing of the entire manuscript, towards the final stage, would have been impossible. Then there is the late Mrs. Ihuoma Igwe of our Theatre Arts Department, University of Jos, with a beloved concern, on this work. Evangelist Joe Ojochide did the musical score. I am grateful.

By for, the greatest contribution in the supply of related literature came from one of my University of Jos pioneering students Miss Clara (Claire) Effiong. I am deeply appreciative.

After the publisher's readers report, came this final professional retyping of the entire manuscript by Mr. Godfrey Anyanwu and the Franco Enterprise, Jos. I am indebted to their commitment.

Sonny Oti,
University of Jos,
Jos,
NIGERIA.

# Foreword

### 'God's Not God of Confusion'

*- Tony Okoroji, President PMAN*

**W/C:** In your press conference you said the life you lived as PMAN President in the past four years has been very frugal. Why do you then want to contest for a third-term and live yet another two years of frugal existence?

**OKOROJI:** It has become obvious to me that there are certain forces that are very desperate to hijack PMAN for their own end. Unfortunately some of our members are being used. There is a danger that this association will be dragged back to square one if we allow the forces to succeed. While it will be the most comfortable thing for me to walk away, I looked back at the efforts that have made PMAN of today possible and I believe that it will be a disaster for Nigerian musicians if PMAN is allowed to crumble. It will be a bigger disaster for our generation of Nigerians because PMAN in the list four years has been an important generation statement. This is why I have decided to make yet another sacrifice of frugal existence.

**W/C:** Your challenger claims that God spoke to her to contest for PMAN Presidency. Did God also speak to you?

**OKOROJI:** The God that we have is God of everybody. And the God I know is not a partial God. He is not the God of falsehood or destruction or of confusion. I am sure that God is behind the progress that PMAN has made over the years and I don't think it is the wish of God to see PMAN destroyed.

**W/C:** You talked about forces that are desperate to hijack PMAN for their own end, can you elaborate on this?

**OKOROJI:** There are people who have very strong financial interests in PMAN and they believe that as long as Tony Okoroji is there, his principles are so strong that he cannot be manipulated and they are behind some candidates who they believe are more sympathetic to their interest. This is why they cooked up all the smear campaign against me, hoping that they will create distrust between me and members of the association. But it is becoming again more and more obvious that they have failed because musicians are no fools. I would not want to name names.

**W/C**: There is the impression that the Federal Government gave the ₦5 million to PMAN because of your personality. How true is this?

**OKOROJI**: PMAN has been here before now and with all modesty, I have no doubt that whatever recognition and support that PMAN has received in the last four years has been because people have confidence in the leadership of PMAN. And this confidence is a result of the fact that each time we say something, we do it, and we don't beat about the bush. While some of us work day and night some people sleep in their homes wanting to claim credit at the end of the day. They can claim credit but they should do nothing to stop the PMAN revolution because the forces of the revolution are too strong for them.

For me the success that we achieved is the success of all of us. It is unfortunate that some small minded people see it as the success of one man, and then decide to fight that one man, so that they can tell everyone no one else can do it but them.

**W/C**: There is the belief that the land that is reportedly allocated to PMAN for the plaza is just a cooked up rumour.

**OKOROJI**: I know that the allocation has been approved and I have seen the papers. The Governor of Lagos State, Col. Raji Rasaki has directed that all necessary details be worked out, and I have implicit trust that the PMAN Plaza will be built and Nigerians will see it go into the skyline.

**W/C**: Talking about the PMAN Plaza, it is believed that you are contesting for the third time because you wanted to take all the credit for the plaza. How true is this?

**OKOROJI**: I am not a man that is interested in projects. I am a man that is interested in getting the work done. Yes the PMAN Plaza is one of the reasons I am contesting because I have got strong vibes that if we are not careful, the funds meant for the Plaza which we have kept away safely will be diverted to some very frivolous uses. Maybe you do not know that PMAN has no property anywhere in Nigeria and that the National Secretariat operates from a rented apartment after we were driven away from another one for failure to pay rents accumulated when my colleague Christy Essien

Igbokwe was treasurer of the union. It is very big source of embarrassment to members of PMAN and they are determined to own their own property that nobody can drive them away from, which can also provide revenue for the association because it is not everyday that somebody will donate ₦5 million to you. And if anybody cannot see the wisdom in building our house on the rock instead of putting our resources in quicksand, I feel sorry for the person.

**W/C**: The PMAN constitution does not specify a limit for the number of tenures any incumbent is qualified to run for re-election. Do you intend to change this if re-elected?

**OKOROJI**: I think that no individual can amend the constitution. My feeling is that despite the provision of the constitution, at the end of the day, the musicians would decide who should be president. Considering that you are going to go back to the members to ask them to vote for you, I don't consider it necessary. But if the combined wisdom of the members decide otherwise, I am a democrat.

*Weekend Concord*, Saturday, 28 October 1991, pages 11 and 14.

# Memory Lane

### A Cull

...the young children, who are always interested in music, also have their own style, called Atikatika...the recent development which has swept through Dagbon._(in Ghana) the Atikatika children are known for singing witty political songs; several times they have been in trouble with local authorities and the national government...

John Miller Chernoff
*African Rhythm and African Sensibility.*

# Contents

*Dedication*   *v*
*Acknowledgements*   *vi*
*Foreword*   *viii*
*Memory Lane: Cull*   *xi*
*Title song: Chioma*   *xiii*

| | | |
|---|---|---|
| Chapter 1 | Introduction: Yesterday: the Movement and the Monument | 1 |
| Chapter 2 | Balladism, Pan-Africanism, and Militarism | 19 |
| Chapter 3 | E.I. Mensah and Ghana's Repertory | 33 |
| Chapter 4 | Blowing their own trumpets | 45 |
| Chapter 5 | Jottings from the Author's diary | 135 |
| Chapter 6 | Conclusion | 143 |
| *Appendix* | | 154 |
| *Index* | | 157 |

# Chioma
-a title song-
(Igbo-English)


Halelujah, Chioma;
Helelujah, Excellent God;
*Onye kere madu, ke olu ya;*
Who created man and his voice;
*K'ayi kwe ukwe, tee egwu;*
That we may sing and dance;
*K'ayi bulie aha gi elu;*
That we may lift your name higher;
*Onye nagwo-oria, akelem gi;*
The Great Physician, I thank you;
*Onye nenye uba, ekelem gi;*
The author of prosperity and wealth,
I greet you;
*Onye ebube na amara, ekelem gi;*
The author of miracles, signs and wonders,
I greet you;
*Ike kacha ike, ekelem gi;*
The super-power over powers, I greet you.

A cull from the album: FAVOUR! of Sonny Oti & The Never Give Up Voices.

# 1

# Introduction

## Yesterday: the Movement and the Monument

Although highlife music belongs to the entertainment genre, it is essentially an urban music. Its dynamism does not lie in the aesthetics of its form and style, as a dance music relying almost totally on western musical instruments; it lies more in its song-texts. Critics evaluate it as a popular music genre, but fail to emphasize that its critical song-texts are the major forces guaranteeing its development and interplay with factors which contribute to the search for even political as well as economic, and national growth and stability in Africa.

Highlife musicians may be referred to as modern African town-criers whose messages or song-texts, like drama and theatre texts, present not only Africa's culture but her social, economic and political problems.

The growing sophistication of highlife song-texts (seen not just as the usual protest songs of freedom airs) influences the beauty or austereness of their rhythms. Experiments aimed at developing highlife music traditional forms to contemporary admixture of old and new, were based on research as carried out by its operators.

The intriguing thing to emphasize is that although a good majority of highlife music operators are not products of formal western music colleges or institutions, they recognize the need for them to carry out field work to collect materials useful to the growth of their song-texts and rhythms. This has led to a significant improvement on the quality and popularity of their works. Both the quality and popularity of their works have resulted in the occasional mini-Grammy award-like ceremonies in which presentations are made to honour the most popular musicians who have recorded great commercial success. Such presentations are done by international and sometimes, local music interests and industrialist. Such recognition and souvenirs are hardly the kind of rewards their western-trained professional counterparts receive.

Western-trained professional musicians hardly acquire as many "gold discs and platinum" as the other class of musicians who use local apprenticeship and intensive exposure of their talents as a catapult to the heights. For instance, Mr Ebenezer Olasupo Fabiyi, *alias* Chief Commander Obey, of the modem juju music, has so far been awarded nineteen gold discs and one platinum; Chief Osita Osadebe of the popular *Oyelima* highlife music, received a double award of two gold discs and a platinum in 1984; whereas what Fela Anikulapo-Kuti gets is either police-baton, custody, court action or clash with the establishment. Upon graduation the western-trained professional opts either to be absorbed by the establishment or remain independent and free to explore the growth of music through entertainment. And it is on the latter's visionary innovations, dynamism, radicalism and experiments that the survival and growth of highlife music depends.

It is true, though, that even since the late forties and early fifties, the "moderated" or "non-radicals" had already established the significance of song-texts. With the idiom, proverbs and philosophies of their peoples, they continued to make appreciable impact on African literature. They remained socially and politically alert. Some masked their political convictions in their "non-aligned" lyrics. Unfortunately, there has been a dearth of specialized critics because what we have around are reviewers who seem unaware of the fact that without its song-texts, highlife is a mere aesthetic skeleton. Even its commercial circulation is determined more by the power of its song-texts than the rhythm and beat which are considered inevitable flavouring spice.

The presence of radicals and Pan-Africanists from the fifties in music has therefore lifted highlife musicians from the status of mere entertainers and nerve therapists to a more serious and responsible one, as African modern town-criers whose song-texts are communal messages, warning and counselling. Even, militant criticisms of the establishment are innovative. The musicians also alert the society on topical issues of significance as the press and the theatre do.

There is currently an appreciable transformation and "transfiguration" in highlife music. Its conventional dancers are giving way to audiences; because the highlife musicians preach political and social messages instead of the passion of dance in their audience. Thus, ears and the mind are now becoming more important, intellectually, than the sensual eyes and body ballroom motion; even the gospel songs like those of Brothers Emmanuel and Lazarus captioned, "Voice of The Cross" are regaining their piety, and may be danced to only as part of church worship. The night clubs themselves, now "disco-oriented", are giving way to live-theatre stages, the stadia and other concert arena for performances of highlife music.

Many dance forms associated with highlife are being revitalized or created by the musicians. Efik *ekombi* was revitalized by Inyang Henshaw; Victor Uwaifo created *akwete, ekassa, sasakosa, mutaba, titibiti,* and *joromi*; Osita Osadebe designed *oyelima*; Sonny Okosun recreated *Ozzidism*; Oriental Brothers invented *ikwokirikwo*; Fela Anikulapo-Kuti created *Afro-beat*. But, while their dance forms depreciate because they lack a "unifying aesthetic force," the song-texts appreciate because they possess the dynamics for oneness and growth as evident in the identifiable serious mood of the lyrics with their common themes of poverty, domestic apartheid and invocations.

Since 1947, the goal of those we have tagged 'Western cultural pop music adherents' in this study has been to level up with the pop art of western culture. They started by attempting to wed Western culture to indigenous ones and, perhaps, prove the universality of the art of dance music to westerners.

The experimentations of western cultural pop music adherents with jazz, its prototype and offshoots, lasted effectively within the fifties, and collapsed. The jazz shows of Bobby Benson; the *ofege* shows of St. Gregory College Boys, Lagos, are examples. Upon the ruins of jazz in Nigeria, highlife music evolved in its dynamic form. Upon the ruins of European clubs in West Africa, particularly in Ghana and Nigeria, highlife gained its lyrical independence to join the indigenous political bandwagon and its crash movement towards freedom. In other words, highlife music was really a by-product of multi-dimensional movements and factors such as showbiz, nationalism, patriotism, musicians, personal frustrations and aspirations, as well as "domestic apartheid." By "domestic apartheid" we mean the artificial class-hierarchy created by African new breed of rich businessmen which replaced the colonial privileged and unprivileged classes. Highlife music emerged from such traditional sources as *juju, osibi, itembe, okombo or asiko, gwoje, kpanlogo, kora, ojojo, nkwanwite, iyambe,* and so forth.

The founding of highlife dance-bands in Ghana was accidental and resulted from racial segregation. British "paternalism" encouraged "mini-apartheid" in their colonies with the existence of European clubs, European hospitals, etc. There was, by this practice, a kind of racial segregation. It was the existence of a European club that indirectly give rise to the formation of the original Tempos Band of Ghana in 1948. And, according to Kwasi Aduonum, The Tempos Band "performed at the European Club at weekends, under the leadership of a British employee of Bartholomew and Company. Harriman and his colleagues, Adolf Doku, Saka Acquaye, Joe Kelley, Ron Kwofie, Bob Hughes and Guy Warren." That was one year after E.T. Mensah's apprenticeship to Leopard of the Army in 1947. And 1947 was also the year Bobby Benson returned to Nigeria from his study trip and service to America and England. Also, 1948 was the year Bobby Benson set up his Bobby-Cassandra show and the jam-session and thus introduced professional "showbiz" to Nigeria. The coincidence of the year 1947 vis-a-vis the origin of African highlife music is significant. It is also worthy of note that Hubert Ogunde's African Music Research Party, according to Ebun Clark, was rechristened, in the year 1947, to Ogunde Theatre Party and that was the company he took to the Gold Coast (Ghana) in 1948 with the concert show "Swing the Jazz". Thus, the prototype of modern "poetic" highlife song-texts was already being developed informally in Ogunde's concert party.

If Nigeria takes the credit for being the first to introduce professional musicians to the art of popular city music, thus evolving highlife-jazz, Ghana would make a justifiable claim to being the first to introduce modern highlife upon which the growth of highlife would depend. In Nigeria, Bobby Benson's group was packed with potential stars: Zeal Onyia, Baby-Face Paul, Victor Olaiya, Eddie Okonta, Roy Chicago, Rex Lawson, Bill Friday, Inyang Henshaw, Rex Williams. Sammy Akpabot (later to become a professor and musicologist) and Bala Miller shared interest in music and were close to Bobby Benson. All Stars Band was a contemporary of Bobby Benson's 'Jam Session Orchestra.' Chris Ajilo, who was running his own band in London, was even persuaded to return to Nigeria and join the pioneering efforts. And at one time "Ajilo hair-do" was fashionable in Nigeria.

While the Nigerian pioneers were still experimenting with jazz, E.T. Mensah's reconstituted and revitalized Tempos Band was touring Nigeria in 1951. And it was not until 1952, according to Ebun Clark, that Bobby Benson switched over to full-time music. Upon the departure of his wife and partners 'Cassandras', he packed up his showbiz. Whereas Bobby Benson become a reference point and "uncle" to them all in Nigeria, Ghana's E.T. Mensah became popular with his contemporaries in Ghana and was idolised in Nigeria after the Nigerian tour, particularly in having given highlife harmony, beauty and form, as well as the use of indigenous Ghanaian and Nigerian languages as highlife music idiom. E.T. Mensah's tour created a new image for Ghana's Tempos Band following the break-up of the original Tempos Band, which was caused by "a private musical tour of Liberia" by "Joe Kelley, Guy Warren and Ron Kwofie" all of the original 'Tempos Band'.

During the forties, both in Nigeria and Ghana, the existence of European clubs posed a challenge which produced local elite. Although these elite initiated the founding of corresponding African clubs, their goal was neither patriotic nor nationalistic. Their objective was selfish and self-centred. African clubs were to serve as recreation fora for Africans who would have wished to be Europeans. Their view was evident in their snobbish attitude towards early forms of highlife. According to Bassey Ita, highlife music was regarded by them as mere folklorish. Native waltz, foxtrot, tango, etc., were ballroom specialities, even in African clubs. Local Victor Sylvesters (during the era of jazz and tap dance) and local Fred Astaires, emerged. Some of these African leisure-oriented elite seemed unaware of the general political wind, mood, movements and rhythms in Africa.

With a growing political consciousness, highlife music later became at the ballroom dance racial clubs, an I.D. card of the West African indigenous elite. It became the "anthem" of the indigenous elite. It became a nationalistic status symbol and a slogan for equal rights. As the tempo of nationalism and patriotism increased with accelerated motion, European clubs collapsed, giving way to inter-racial clubs, otherwise christened 'Recreation Clubs.' Here, highlife music was danced to, even by Europeans, who performed on the dance floor as if they were engaged in the athletic event of hop-step-and-jump. But, of relevance was the fact that the backs of paternalism and racism were broken. Also, interaction between the races, in the public, became acceptable but the tilt was merely from race to class; and that was where the stigma of domestic-apartheid surfaced after independence, and became one of the targets of radical highlife song-texts.

On the Nigerian scene, Rex Lawson popularized the philosophies and languages of the Kalabari and Ijaw peoples; Inyang Henshaw expertly underlined Efik idioms and literature; Victor Uwaifo propagated the historical excellence of Bini culture and Osita Osadebe not only highlighted the richness of Igbo proverbs but produced and influenced an outstanding corpus of stars (Osadebe himself was a product of Stephen Amechi), who have stamped their own personalities on the style and form of his *Oyelima* highlife music. The out-growth of Osadebe's *Oyelima* highlife include "*Ikenga-Ikwakirikwo*" of Ikenga Superstars, Oriental Brothers International Band and Paulson Kalu. Fela Anikulapo-Kuti introduced a trilingual song-text (Yoruba, English,

Pidgin) to his *Afro-beat*. Even in the late fifties and early sixties, Victor Olaiya had experimented, not only with his native Yoruba language, but also with Igbo and Efik, utilizing his exposure to the languages of some states east of the Niger. Israel Nwoba and his "Three Night Wizards" even earlier than Olaiya, had exposed the delicious characteristics of Owerri dialect of *Ndi Igbo* in his ballad-highlife music. Joe Nez used Owerri dialect effectively, too, about the same period.

Hausa language has been used from time to time even by Victor Olaiya, but has never really concretized as a regular highlife song-text language because of under-use. Later, Bala Miller, who was the principal of the only Nigerian professional music school, founded by him for Kano State government in Nigeria, re-opened the use of Hausa language in highlife song-texts in the seventies. Upon the death of the military Governor of Kano State, Alhaji Audu Bako, the school was closed down. Before his position at the School of Music, Bala Miller was a top executive of a number of commercial firms at one time or the other. When the School of Music was no longer operational, he opted for developing music and musicians on his own financial resources. He acquired the Kaduna-based Costain Club and converted it into a nightclub. He gave it a resident band which operates an African "ballroom" dance-band that he directs. The band is Pan-Africanist in its membership, comprising Camerounians, Ghanaians, Gambians, etc. On the platform of his night-club, and on the stage of his African Pyramids Band, Bala Miller has been trying to make Hausa language an idiom for highlife music. The inference here is that Nigerian highlife music should not appear to have waited for external inspirations in order to exploit fully and consistently the richness of indigenous languages.

In Ghana, an endless quest for aesthetics in highlife music was responsible for the production of dance and guitar bands which could each claim stardom. The dance bands included Black Beats Band, Stargazers Dance Band, Onyina Guitar Band, Broadway Dance Band, Red Spots Band, Ramblers International Band, Akompi's Guitar Band, E.K.'s Band, E.T. Mensah & His Tempos Band, The Republicans, Spike Anyakor's Regimental, Police, Railway Silver Band and Professional Uhuru. From the fifties to early sixties, the works of these bands dominated Nigerian records market to the extent that it became fashionable for Nigerian dance bands to recruit Ghanaian vocalists to sing the most popular songs of Ghana's top highlife dance bands, in Nigerian night-clubs. To maintain the lead, Ghanaian bands recruited some Nigerian musicians to enable them write songs in Nigerian languages. As a result, 'Black Beats' produced two masterpieces in

Nigerian languages: one was in Yoruba with the title "*Owo ko ni fé*", the other was in Efik "*Abasi do*". And, incidentally, "*Abasi do*" scratches the theme of infatuation:

> *Ekpri ediye cyan anwan*
> *Okwut mi k'usung*
> *Okom mi monyong*
> *Ono mi leta*
> *Obup ima*
> *Abasi do*
> *Ami ntongo erong kisong*
> *mbong akam*
> *Akwa Abasi anam nkpo*

E.T. Mensah & his Tempos Band also produced two popular ones in Efik. The titles were "*Keyere Mong*" and "*Calabar*".

By early sixties, Rex Lawson's highlife music excelled itself to the extent that many Nigerians "transferred" Rex Lawson's "citizenship" to Ghana. Even his Kalabari/Ijaw language was mistaken, by some Nigerians, to be Akan, Ga, Ewe, or Twi languages of Ghana. The rise of Rex Lawson and the quality of Ghanaian highlife music have a bearing on the following accounts.

Sigma Club of Ibadan University annually organized a carnival that was evaluated as "the most popular in West Africa". Sigma Club was not just an elitist students' club, it was a responsible one and was highly respected. Both the Vice-Chancellor and the Registrar of the institution were usually honorary members, whose oath of membership was, conventionally, administered by the student Sigma Chief. The club, in spite of its lofty values, was not snobbish.

The club, in fact, established a "scholarship" programme for non-Sigmites. Selection for qualification of the award, given the charitable objective, was administered by the University of Ibadan upon the request of the benefactors.

About seven dance bands were selected by the club annually to cover varying interests and ages during the colourful carnival named 'Havana Nite'. The most current popular band in West Africa took the Tower-Court pavilion, which was the most prestigious band-stand of Nigeria's premier University. The club's carnival may be regarded as the forerunner of Top-of-the-Chart organization in West Africa. So popular was the carnival that it attracted a good breed of people even from Sierra Leone.

In a way, Sigma Club generated a competitive movement for West

African highlife dance bands towards excellence. For many years, the most popular highlife dance band came from Ghana. Nigerian bands, like Victor Olaiya, E. C. Arinze's and Stephen Amechi's 'Empire Rhythm Orchestra' played in alternating turns with the Ghanaian bands. That was the first sign of recognition for Nigerian bands by the club. But between early and mid-sixties, a political accident would completely change the policy of Sigma Club's selection of dance bands for Havana Nite.

In spite of a strained political relationship between Ghana and Nigeria, Sigma Club still selected Ramblers International Dance Band of Ghana as the most popular then on the West Coast of Africa. Mr. Pip Edorhe, who was both an executive of Sigma Club and also President of Ibadan University's Students Union, was sent to Ghana. He was to negotiate with Ramblers Band for the Havana Nite of 1964. The press at Accra airport insisted on his opinion as President of the leading students union in Nigeria about the Nigeria-Ghana political feud. Mr. Edorhe took a "patriotic stand" on behalf of Nigeria. That cost him his mission; Ramblers would no longer be available. His attempt to contract Ramblers Band became fruitless. He was told that Mr Jerry Hansen, the leader of the band, was airborne for England to do some studies. He was also made to understand that as a result of Mr. Hansen's absence, Ramblers Band was not performing but it was all a political game devoid of any truth. Of course, Mr Edorhe had no option to his press statement in Ghana during the "Ant-Elephant" political verbal duel between Ghana and Nigeria.

That incident became an epoch; it augured favourably for the image of Nigerian highlife dance bands because it influenced the policy of the Sigma Club. Rex Lawson stepped, competently and expertly, into the vacuum created by Ramblers Dance Band of Ghana and was Havana Nite's number one dance band that year. Rex Lawson proudly set up at the Tower-Court band-stand.

That Sigma Club's annual carnival had made a vital impact on the development of dance bands may partly be evaluated from the curriculum vitae of a Nigerian superstar, Victor Uwaifo. In 1983, he was presented the prestigious Nigerian National Honours of "Member of the Order of the Niger (M.O.N)", by the civilian head of state and Commander-in-Chief of Nigerian Armed Forces, Alhaji Aliyu Shehu Shagari. Victor Uwaifo's citation proudly included the listing of the award presented him by Sigma Club. It read "Grand Order of the Havana (G.O.H), University of Ibadan, Sigma Club" (among his other international awards and honours).

By the late sixties and early seventies, stardom in highlife music switched over from Ghana to Nigeria. Victor Uwaifo arrived in Ghana with his new "*Joromi*" and "*Akwete*" highlife, as well as his 24-string double-neck electric guitar (the 24-string was his own invention). His "*Joromi*" and "*Guitar Boy*" song-texts introduced an innovation. His traditional exhibitionism on his guitar, played not only with his fingers, but with virtually every part of his body, established his claim to being a "guitar-boy". His popularity on Ghanaian soil broke Ghana's stardom "monopoly" in highlife. Even Ghana's army labelled "an attempted counter-coup" which took place on 17 April 1967 as "operation Guitar Boy". That coup under Lieutenant Samuel Arthur led to the death of General Kotoka during its execution. Thus, so popular was Victor Uwaifo in Ghana that even his "*Joromi* costume" became fashionable there.

The next Nigerian musician to make a significant and magical incursion in Ghana was Fela Anikulapo-Kuti and his Afro-Beat. His was not even a self-programmed tour of Ghana; it was an official trip. He was invited, royally, to do a command performance for Ghana's military head of state, Lieutenant Colonel I. K. Achampong. But, since Fela was essentially 'a man of the people,' his reception spread until it got to the grassroots. It was a scene of hero-worship in Ghana because his music was not only of high audio appeal, it was also a sophisticated package of sound and ideology. His group was enlarged by Ghanaian adherents among who was a young lawyer who not only returned with him to Nigeria, but camped with him and Africa 70 in Fela's temporary "Kalakuta Republic" residence at Ikeja.

A critic observed that Fela Anikulapo-Kuti's Afro Beat is the pulse of African music before Bob Marley. Both Bob Marley and Fela shared the vision of song-texts as media and dynamic force for communicating Africa's (Black people's) social, economic and political problems. Of course, Jamaica and Trinidad have continued to use lyrics as "a nuclear weapon of attack and defence" against the oppressors of the black and African peoples of the Third World in general. Both Jamaica and Trinidad have produced Pan-Africanists, even in music. This is reminiscent of the pioneering work of a barrister from Trinidad named H. Sylvester Williams who coined the term "Pan-Africa.' That coinage influenced "the father of Pan Africanism, William Du Bois. Jamaica herself was the home of Marcus Garvey who, in 1914 in New York, called himself "Leader of the Negro Peoples of the World" and used as his slogan 'Africa for the Africans'. These were the peers whose "artist-politician" off-springs comprise, among others, Mighty Sparrow, Bob Marley, Jimmy Cliff and Peter Tosh.

Bob Marley's "radicalism" and the "Pan Africanism" of Peter Tosh and Jimmy Cliff have continued to complement African voices and African rhythms, through their protest songs - in the case they make on behalf of Africa and the Third World who are still exploited politically and economically especially by the western world.

From Bob Marley, we see the Jamaican-Caribbean's common goal with African homeland. We see artists from the roots, and the kindred from the homeland impatient with exploiters and materialists. In "Exodus" and "Survival," Bob Marley jeers:

> How can you be sitting there
> Telling me that you care
> That you care
> When every time I look around
> The people suffer in suffering
> In every where. In every where

Bob Marley also mobilizes public conscience as he campaigns:

> Are you satisfied
> with the life you are living?
> Move
> Move
> Move
> Move
> Move
> Move
> Exodus - Movement of the people...
> Don't bury your thoughts
> Put your vision to reality
> Life is one big road with lots of signs
> So when you are rising thru the ruts

And, as if he would resign it all to fate, he thinks aloud:

> In this age of technological inhumanity...
> Scientific atrocity...
> atomic mis-philosophy
> a world that forces
> life-long insecurity ...
> Nothing change
> Nothing strange

But, then, he is confident that the survival of the African and the black man is assured, in spite of all the odds posed by racial superiority complex and bullying. Like James Brown, Bob Marley declares that he is proud to be a black of African roots. As a 'Rastaman', he believes in Jah and holds that he is son of Fire. That fire which can melt gold and set materialists and racists in panic, while the children of Rastamen are at peace with life secured under Jah's protective powers:

> We are the children of Rastaman
> We are the children of Fireman
> I know that Jah will not let us down...

Under Jah's parental security, Bob Marley is able to take a fresh look at the stampede of the materialists. He sneers:

> See them fighting for power
> But they know not the hour
> They keep us hungry
> When you gonna get some food
> Your brother got to be your enemy...
> Ambush in the night...
> Everywhere the fire's burning
> Every day we are fighting
> They make the world so hard
> The people are dying
> From hunger and starvation...
> Babylon's system is vampire
> Sucking the children day by day
> They are sucking the blood of the sufferer...

Bob Marley then pedals back into history and spirituality:

> I'll never forget no way they
> Crucified Jesus Christ...
> I'll never forget no way they
> Sold Marcus Garvey...
> When the rain fails, it falls
> On one man's house...
> Many more will have to suffer Many more will have to
> die Don't ask me why
> I don't tell no lies...

His conclusion is significant because it guides us to understand the strategy, logistics, and gimmicks of apartheid:

> So they bribing
> With their guns, spare parts and money
> Trying to belittle our integrity
> We're not ignorant. I mean it...
> You see them sailing in their ego trips
> Blest off in their space-ships
> Million miles from reality
> No care for you, No care for me...
> So my brethren, my sisthren
> The preaching and talking is done...

But it is not "done". Nigerian Sonny Okosun takes the song-text relay baton. We see him preaching from a political soapbox, and presenting a power sermon to stir up the spirit of his compatriots and Pan-Africanists. He captions his text "My Papa's Land":

> Chinese are ruling the Chinese lands;
> Japan is ruled by Japanese;
> England is govern by Englishmen
> America, governed by Americans;
> We must rule from
> Cape to Cairo
> We must rule
> Our Papa's land

The uneven distribution of wealth, in developing countries, is an index of the regular economic depression of the economically disadvantaged peoples of the world. Neo-colonialism continues to ensure that Africa remains politically immature. As far as the neo-colonialists are concerned, the frequency of coup d'états in Africa, which could stagnate initiatives in indigenous industrial revolution, is an index of Africa's political immaturity. In other words, they would be happy to watch African political "retrogressive game" of regular reverse motion to the starting point. But the indication is that the extraordinary situations in Africa may depend on extraordinary measures and disciplines of a sweeping revolution to establish stabilized political and economic base for African home-lands and nations.

This political state of affairs has increased the sensitivity of Africa's rhythms and musical pendulum – poverty clashes with apartheid, the options seem limited. The by-product which follows, as a result of resignation and helplessness, is innovative texts which appeal for home-cleansing, mobilization of all available resources and invocation, not only to the god of technology, but also to Almighty God, the Supreme Deity.

After the collapse of the experiments on African-Western cultural equilibrium by the first generation of western pop music adherents, led by Bobby Benson, a "roosting" period intervened. The next active incursion, by foreign rhythms, had to wait until the seventies when a school-boy rock group led by Melvin Ukachi and named "*Ofege*" emerged with their "Try and Love" album. The source was the same St. Gregory College, Lagos, which produced Mike Enahoro and Victor Uwaifo.

During the Nigerian Civil War years, a Western pop music adherent's team led by Eddie Roberts had emerged in mid-sixties but they shifted their operation to "Biafra". Jake Solo, who later distinguished himself in the London-based '*Osibisa*', was a member of Eddie Roberts 'Hykker's International'. Pat Fin (Okonji), and Ify Jerry were all in Hykkers International.

In early seventies, a rock group, named "The Strangers" produced a sensational piece called "Love Rock". It competed favourably with sounds from abroad. "The Wings" attracted the attention of critics. Then "Mono-Mono" group made it with their single "Give a Beggar a Chance". The "Sweet Breeze" rock group did not forget African culture with African roots. "The Apostles", based at Aba in Nigeria, joined the Western pop music adherents' bandwagon. It is important to note that even before contemporary western-oriented pop musicians like Theodora Ifudu, Onyeka Onwenu and Tony Grey saw the need for cultural flavouring in their works, the Hykkers International had already led the way in the sixties.

In spite of the above, it is important to note that the song-texts of African culture did not formally associate themselves with Africa's social and cultural thesis. It appears that they were all along misguided towards stardom, cash and commercial successes abroad (which was dictated by curious patronage). Yet, they may have wished to identify themselves with the struggles and aspirations of their developing nations. Perhaps, they had hoped, with sincerity, to wed African drum to western synthesizer, thereby neutralizing the monopoly of the West in technological pop art. Could their efforts be regarded negative or complementary and challenging in the face of events in Africa?

Is it possible to re-make their world? Jimmy Cliff appears to have used a Supreme Military Council musical base to issue decrees in a military answer to the wishes of African-Western pop music adherent. Jimmy Cliff directs:

> Re-make the world;
> Be you Black, be you White;
> Remake the world
> With Love and Happiness
> Put your conscience to the test
> Too many people are suffering
> Too many people are sad
> Too many people got everything
> While too many people got nothing
> Too little people got everything
> While the good suffer for the bad

The more racial and class consciousness produced bigotry, the more song-texts miffed the hearts of diplomatic forces. Peter Tosh satirizes the futility of human pretext to acquire a place of sanctity in that beyond named "Paradise" without putting their earthly home in order:

> Everyone wants to get to heaven
> But none of them wants to die
> Everyone wants to get to the top
> But tell me how far it is from the bottom

A hint of optimism follows as Jimmy Cliff urges "Struggling Man:"

> Struggling Man have a right to live
> Struggling Man, has got to move
> Struggling Man, no time to lose...
> To higher heights...
> Better days are coming by and by...

As African highlife rhythm song-texts transform into rhetoric and discourse and the past, the present, and the future of Africa, a crystallization of a realistic union of the black people, dreamt by some black political radicals, like Marcus Garvey, Osagyefo Kwame Nkrumah and others, begin to emerge. We find it emerging in the "ballard world" ahead of the "real world" where Africans still struggle, suffer and smile. With the growing seriousness of the song-texts, we notice a movement towards identification with less entertaining forces which are relevant to nationhood in Africa. The patriotic and nationalistic commitment of African musicians crystallizes more effectively as they use the vehicle of serious entertainment to participate in "the push" and "the move". Eventually, they would lift Africa and win multi-racial fans.

No track title could probably be more appropriate than that coined for Quincy Jones' production of superstars in USA captioned "We Are The World". The charity-album "USA For Africa" was done to generate funds as relief for victims of natural disaster and allied misfortunes in Africa. In "We are The World", the world of musicians transcends the material world of racists, negrophobists and anti-white movements. If either Diana Ross or Michael Jackson were declared the "President of the World", it would take a while before their multi-racial citizens woke up to the fact of their race, if they do. The same would apply to Kenny Rogers or Dolly Parton and other superstars whose works Africans and the Third World patronize fanatically, regardless of their colour.

## Institutional vectors

We cannot discuss the history of highlife music in any meaningful way or even hold that song-texts are, in a way, parallels of classroom lectures unless we identify the institutions responsible for documenting and circulating nightclub rhetorics (lyrics) through gramophone records and recorded cassette tapes. We may not even assume that we can see beyond the entertainment facade of highlife music and its musicians unless we undertake an excursion of the operations of the archives which preserve their contributions.

Recording companies in Nigeria established a triple role as talent scouts, record manufacturers and preservers of disc documents since the late fifties. Without the experiments of the early years, the fallen stars of yester-years would have left behind only a fragile monument. The stars of today would have no hopes to guide them towards a tomorrow of optimism socially, politically, economically and even culturally. Recording companies succeeded to create musical monuments.

In Nigeria, musicians, like press-men, were referred to as "The Boys". This was a loaded nomenclature which even implied that both music and journalism were not professions for women. "The Boys" also implied a tag which could mean "glorified servants" or "our entertainers" or even a group which belongs to a comic profession of "lay-abouts" because they were only pawns who may be manipulated by the "established masters". Thus, arrogant patronage was involved. But that arrogance was veiled by fear and respect because musicians, theatre-artists, press men and artists in general have in their possession the trump card whose devastating and mobilization effect the masters were aware of. Paradoxically, because of the masters' patronizing stance and their recognition of the unpublicized powers of these under-dogs, musicians were not accorded a place of honour nationally within contemporary urban setting.

Bobby Benson of Nigeria and E. T. Mensah of Ghana severally fought for recognition for the image of musicians and their contributions towards the socio-political growth of the society. Bobby Benson made sure he never begged for food and cash. He established himself as a master and developed a forum to build up and encourage his contemporaries towards self reliance.

E. T. Mensah quit a reputable profession of pharmacy for a career in the popular music of highlife. At that time, it was an adventure loaded with economic risks and social hazards. But E.T.'s (as he was popularly referred to) decision underlined a choice of conviction in careerism. Of course, in the late forties, performing arts was an ignoble career. But in the end, E. T. Mensah, through his song-texts, was recognized as one who could influence political thoughts and alignments not only in Ghana but also in other parts of Africa.

I. K. Dairo, a juju-music maestro, was honoured in the early years; but that was an exception. He was not political; thus his lyrics did not threaten the establishment. His social-satirical comments, as well as his revolutionary and innovative dimensions to modernize juju-music, could not be ignored. He was thus awarded the British colonial honours of O.B.E. (Order of the British Empire).

As colonial citizens, some Nigerian citizens received British Empire awards like O.B.E. which some Nigerian fundamentalist nationalists derided with the tag of "Obedient Boy of The Empire". There were other titles like K.B.E., K.C.M.G. (Knight Commander of St. Michael and St. George), etc. Under this title, Dr Francis Akanu Ibiam was knighted by Queen Elizabeth II of England. But Sir Francis was surprisingly a sincere reputable radical, a recognized world church leader. The crisis which led to the Nigerian Civil War (named Biafran War) also led Sir Francis Ibiam to shed his knighthood and erase the accolade in disagreement with British diplomacy on the eve of the war. He stripped his name both of the "Sir-ship" and the foreign Christian first name to remain Dr. Akanu Ibiam.

Currently, the award of National Honours in Nigeria has justified her independent status which demands the decolonization of the mentality of Nigerian citizenry. There is an attempt to re-define the prerequisites for awards, to re-define the spectrum of recipients. The result of such re-definition could be pre-empted. From the genesis of awards, quality-oriented conservatism which guided the awards would be retained, while liberalism attendant on post-colonial national policy programmes would be reflected across board by abrogating prejudices which hitherto relegated certain careers, professions and vocations to the background.

Already, the tag referred to as "The Boys" is disappearing because "The Girls" have joined. Formal education in the profession of music and journalism has also made the tag impotent and obsolete in the established masters' out-dated lexicon.

In spite of all these flashes of a new approach, there are a number of contributors who, no matter the input they make, will continue to hang around the periphery, around the limelight and centre stage. This study is committed to focusing the spotlight on some musicians of highlife, their counterparts and a sample of the operators behind the back-drop, who are sculptors of effigies and images representing tributes to both the fallen stars and the living ones.

The early organizations concerned with improvisational recording of the pioneering performing musicians in Nigeria were Decca, E.M.I., Phillips (West African) Records. The only indigenous company was C.T. Onyekwelu's Nigerphone at Onitsha in Nigeria which was in association with Phillips (West African Record Limited). According to Nkem Ugo Obu, "the company started its Nigerian operations in 1961 with a small office and printing plant jointly owned by it and C.T. Onyekwelu's group."

The cautious strategy of Phillips West African Records in taking shelter under an indigenous company to make its debut on the stage of Nigerian music industry was worthy of a study. Its adaptability to the changing cultural, social and political environment and climate of Nigeria also compels suspicion, attention and critical appraisal because it is a foreign company. Why, unlike a number of other organizations, did it identify itself, rather early, with an indigenous company in Nigeria? Why did it re-christen itself twice, from Phillips West African Records Limited to Phonogram and currently to Polygram Recording Company? How much has the company done to transfer technology to Nigeria in order to identify itself with Nigerian national planning policies which include indigenisation and technology transfer? How far has the company oriented its clientele policies in favour of Nigerian musicians, music industry in Nigeria towards cultural development and popular music business? How much impact has the Performing

Musicians Association of Nigeria (PMAN) made on Polygram Records Company and its counterparts in the Nigerian records industry?

There is evidence of caution, vision, and expertise in the organisation under the company's succeeding chief executives (designated managing directors) right from the early years of Mr. Bond through Mr. Van Leewen (who was the first head of the pioneering department named Gramophone Records under Phillips Nigeria Limited), and Dr. Martijnse to the managing director at the time of writing, Mr. Seyeesener.

Polygram Records Company has "swallowed" Decca the world over except in Nigeria where Decca renamed itself "Afrodesia". Phillips, the Dutch-based parent organisation, has also grown in business strength to the extent that while its German-based partner, Siemens, reduced its share from 50 per cent to 10 per cent at the time, Phillips organizations increased its share in Polygram Records from 50 per cent to 90 per cent.[1]

By licence agreement, Polygram Records Company has the right to market important international artists like the Commodores, Stevie Wonder, The Temptations, Lionel Richie, Marvin Gaye, Oscar, New Edition, Musical Youths, Don Williams, Kenny Rogers and others. Mr. Johnson Adesanya Adenaike confirms that Polygram Records markets the products of giant organizations like W.A., M.C.A., Motown, Sony and others. Polygram Records Company is operational in UK, Belgium, France, Germany, Australia, Greece, USA, Mexico, Argentina, Japan and other major countries of the world.

In spite of the challenges from piracy, which complicates the joys and tears of the music industry, many entrepreneurs in the music industry still breed and exploit music as cosmetic and therapy of emotion and the mind.

A number of local music companies have risen since those heady days: Tabansi at Onitsha, Rogers All-Stars at Awka, Wilrilm at Enugu, Codiac at Enugu, Phonodisk at Ijebu Ode. There is one too at Ibadan, Decca, playing a major pioneering role when gramophone box and fragile 78 r.p.m. discs were in vogue, establishing celebrities like Israel Nwoba, Okonkwo Adigwe (both of blessed memories) and others. Lagos has an outstanding number of local labels and recording companies. E.M.I established superstars like Sonny Okosun whose

---

[1] Since the study was completed in early 1990s, mergers and takeovers have characterized the music industry and as such this account may not truly reflect the state of affairs today. Indeed, many of the recording companies mentioned here may no longer exist or be operating in Nigeria.

image is now international. Generally, their input, even if indirectly, towards the development of a socially, politically, culturally conscious Nigerian and African society, is worthy of a critical attention. But extraordinarily significant is the pragmatic concept of commercial partnership, even at the experimental period, which brought Polygram and C.T. Onyekwelu under a unique association which will later create a wide-based employment opportunity for Nigerians. The level of technological, technical, commercial and industrial training offered to Nigerians within the organizations holds a future either for technology transfer or for technological independence of a kind to Nigeria's music industry.

# 2

# Balladism, Pan-Africanism and Militarism

Is Fela Anikulapo-Kuti a rebel, a radical and revolutionary? Or, is he a confrontationalist, a deviant and an alarmist? Or is he a trouble-maker and a non-conformist? Is he a critic who enjoys threatening established authority? Is he a Pan-Africanist or a champion of Black Power? The answers to these questions may be provided by his song-texts, critiques of his works, his shows, the police, the jail houses, show promoters, recording companies, writers, etc. One thing is certain about him. No one who knows him well enough can ever think of tagging the phrase "criminal" to his name without really disbelieving himself. Even criminals, investigators and prosecutors find it difficult to use the phrase "criminal" along with his name, except that in law there may be no discrimination in conventional jargons and phraseology.

Although his confrontations with established authority usually echoes the image of Nigeria's pioneer dramatist Hubert Ogunde - bringing memorable reflections, Fela Anikulapo-Kuti's name rather invokes the ghost of Israel Nwoba, a renowned balladist of the early fifties.

Israel Nwoba was the vocalist of a group in the early fifties named "Three Night Wizards". He was assassinated after a show by his colleagues, on Thursday, 7 April 1955 on the eve of a Good Friday and that, of course, was a significant date.

Like Fela, Israel changed his surname (from Njemanze to Nwoba) but it was necessitated by a reason which is not parallel to Fela's. Israel dropped his surname fully as a mark of respect for a traditional ruler, the Chief of Owerri, in the defunct Eastern Nigeria. He was a native of that neighbourhood. Both Israel and the traditional ruler, by sheer co-incidence, shared the same surname. Like Fela, Israel was a great satirist. He was very concerned with the cleansing of the African society. He was not a political critic like Fela but he lampooned the society equally in his song-texts. While Fela's song-texts are packed with dynamite and activism, Israel's song-texts had wit and humour which made the listener laugh at himself.

Israel Nwoba was sincere and simple; there was no complexity in his work, yet he was almost "a Moliere transferred". He was as authentic as Fela, but his greatest contribution was that he could be credited with pioneering the dynamism of song-texts at a time when urban popular musicians were still trying to establish the rhythms of the new genre to be named highlife. The Western pop music adherents would rather use the word "sound" as a substitute for highlife. Of course, "sound" is apt for "discotheque" because the rhythms are like the sound of explosives. The early years of highlife was an experiment to produce standardized highlife rhythms whose song-texts, as indicated earlier on, were not a serious input into contemporary issues of national planning policies. Then, E.C. Arinze's "*Va analum okwum*" (They have seduced my girl friend) and Zeal Onyia's "*Vic nyem afum - o*" (Vic, give me back my half-penny) - all of the fifties - are parallels to most song-texts of African cultural bridgeheads like Chris Okotie's, Jide Obi's, Felix Liberty's and their contemporaries of the eighties. Thus, those pioneering years "without song-texts" highlighted Israel Nwoba's contributions in the establishment of critical lyrics.

In Nigeria, the "near vacuum", in terms of a repertoire of lyrics, created by the absence of song-texts, in the early fifties and beyond, became a stimulus to an incursion by foreign discs. Swahili and Zulu song-texts and rhythms dominated the Nigerian popular music market. Lord Kitchener's calypso stabilized and later had a talented Nigerian adherent named Godwin Omabuwa. Congo rhythms and lyrics entrenched their presence. From Lord Kitchener's calypso to those of Mighty Sparrow, we listened to great satires pouring in from the West Indian steel-bands. Even the country music of Tennessee became Nigeria's early morning, late-night and Sunday serenades. Jim Reeves established as the fore-runner of Don Williams. The death of Jim Reeves, following the release of his album "We Thank Thee" in which he sang "This World is Not My Home.." was a near-national grief in Nigeria. The Beetles sound heralded the emergence of local whirlwind pop groups identified with sirenic and screaming voices.

Even in competition with these foreign song-texts, Israel Nwoba's lyrics sustained its jibes beginning with himself, and his tribe:

> You know why I am very short
> You lend me your ears

> And hear why I am short-eh
> My mother is very short
> My father - very short;
> My sisters, all are very short-eh
> And my children
> I suppose they will be short...
> Measuring me
> With the guitar I play
> I am short
> Guitar is short
> I am short
> I am only four feet
> Eleven inches
> All round me very short -a very short-eh
> I am very short – eh
> All round me very short
> Shortness, shortness, shortness - ha!

Then, of course, he lampooned the Igbo women of his tribe as shown elsewhere:

> If you want to make a lover
> Never you make an Ibo woman...

That way, Israel Nwoba became a celebrity as confirmed by the national sorrow which followed his assassination as well as the celebrated court trials of his assassins. Angus Okoli, in his article, in the March issue of 1973 *Headlines* - a monthly newspaper, concludes:

> The jury returned to the chamber. The clock on the wall struck 7.30 a.m. As the condemned men were being taken to the Black Maria for the first lap of their journey to face the hangman's noose, the crowd outside the court jeered. The men were later hanged at the Broad Street prison...

It is relevant to note that Angus Okoli observes:

> Many people would remember him for such recorded songs as "A debtor, e no dey go to prison, only thieves go for jail" and "If you want to make a lover, never make an Ibo woman."

There is also evidence to show that Israel Njemanze held the view that a musician needs formal academic training. One of the factors which led to his assassination was his determination to go abroad for formal training in music:

> Njemanze had already announced his plan to travel to the United Kingdom to study music. On his return, he said, he would build a hotel in Port Harcourt and settle down to play...

It is noteworthy to observe that in 1955, Nigeria was not yet an independent nation, yet the death of Israel Nwoba Njemanze was of national concern to the extent that he was virtually treated as a national hero because of his song-texts and his contribution to popular music as an art whose invaluable input towards the growth of Nigeria was recognized:

> The jury visited the spot where Njemanze's body was found...There was heavy rain that day, crowds very eager to have a glimpse of the accused persons, defied the rain to follow the jury (a 12-man jury headed by Mr. Justice John Benneth). People booed and abused the accused persons...Njemanze was a crowd puller and crowds (always) gathered to listen to him...

Although one is not too sure that the colonial establishment would have identified with fans, to go into all the pains she took, to make sure justice was done, if Israel Njemanze was a political activist in musical costume, yet, the thoroughness in investigations and the composition of the jury which condemned all but two of the accused persons, was testimony enough for the invaluable role of the popular musician in social development. Angus Okoli remarks:

> The trial of the eighteen men arising from the grisly murder that shocked the nation opened before Mr. Justice John Benneth...There were emotional crowd scenes outside the court. Every available seat was taken up in the court room.

As a boy, I recall that I was in Port Harcourt when Israel Nwoba Njemanze died. I saw a mammoth crowd (a group of mourning fans) along Bonny Street carrying an "enlarged" photograph of the musician, chanting dirges. That experience readily comes to mind when I think of the premonitions Israel had before his death as recorded by Angus Okoli:

> In 1922, he showed early interest in music, When he mooted the idea he was to enlist in the army during the Second World War, his mother objected. She said it was a career that was certain to end in untimely death. Israel died in his prime of youth as his mother feared.

Instead of his own popular lyrics, on the night he died, he sang:

> Lord, when thy kingdom comes, remember me.
> Thus spoke the dying lips to dying ears:
> O faith, which in that darkest hour could see
> The promised glory of the far-off years.

Israel Nwoba thus left his footprints on the sands of time as a social commentator. He also left the echoes of his highlife rhythms on the ears of time. He must have converted a number of criminals with his song-texts. He was always willing to behave like a strolling preacher, minstrel and entertainer:

> Njemanze visited his relations at 81 Ibidun Street, Surulere. He drank there and played some of the records his group waxed. He also sang to the pleasure of the tenants...He sang, danced and cracked jokes as he headed towards Surulere roundabout. The crowds followed and cheered.

The moralistic and didactic themes evident in his lyrics will continue to act as jingles for re-ordering the society if one can catch the wit he always employed. "A debtor e no dey go to prison, only thieves go to jail." By this he underlines, "thou shalt not steal" and emphasize man's interaction and dependence on his neighbour debtor; "e no dey go to prison."

Like Bongos Ikwue's "Pick-pocket" track in his album with the title "Lagos" and like this author's song-text named "Lagos Calypso," Israel Nwoba discussed the "mad-rush" in the cities and the criminal acts which result from it. He sang:

> "...The bus reaching at Idi-Oro, everybody went away.

A collector picks up the parcel and then took the parcel to his wife. When the wife opened the parcel, he saw a dead child..."

This author, eight years after Israel Nwoba, in his 1963 "Lagos Calypso" sang:

> You'll find highlife everywhere
> In resorts as Tarkwa Bay
> And multi-coloured nightclubs
> No welcome to racial snubs
> You'll find perfumed mini-skirts
> Combating with stinking air
> Keeping vigil in night clubs
> Sapping victims pockets dry
> Round the corners are cheaters (cheats)
> Smartly dressed but they are pimps
> With an eye on your cocoa notes (cash)
> To make you lighter and wiser
> The narrow streets do no harm
> The inhabitants are full of charm
> Life is fast, business is fast
> And fast grows the traffic jam.

Sonny Okosun veils his popular music with a cultural tag otherwise named "Ozzidism". One sees a combination of reggae and highlife persistent in his sound and rhythms. Yet what is important is that he has established "a corpus of song-texts of propaganda" in defence of Africa and black people and of course, all humanity. In this regard, one sees him as a musical Pan-Africanist. His domestic comments are couched in rhetorics and irony making it safe for him to operate his Pan-Africanism from a secured base. Although he is not a militant like Fela Anikulapo-Kuti and Bob Marley, he has, like Peter Tosh, established a power-base with his song-texts. In Nigeria, his home base, no one talks about "Ozzidism", but many talk about his lyrics "Which Way Nigeria?" or the one before it "Together we shall live forever and forever we shall live together."

Consistently, Israel Nwoba, Inyang Henshaw, Fela Anikulapo-Kuti, Sonny Okosun, Celestine Ukwu and Osita Osadebe rank among those whose songs consumers want to listen to rather than dance to. Although their "sounds" are compelling, yet many would rather settle down and discuss their texts. Although Bongos Ikwue cannot be placed in the development of highlife music, his song-texts are worthy of recognition because his input is not that of an entertainer *per se*, it is that of a societal watchdog and critic.

Since reggae, like calypso, can trace its source to African roots, in spite of other sources, it was possible for Sonny Okosun to absorb it into Ozzidism culture. His early years were reggae-oriented because that was the vogue of the period in Nigeria. The combination of reggae and Ozzidism, with the latter as the senior partner produced reggae – highlife, with a jazz flavour. If reggae influenced the early years of Sonny Okosun's exposure, it also influenced his song-texts. Both calypso and reggae are characterized by satiric and serious song-texts drawing their themes from social and political problems, (like apartheid and negrophobism) neo-colonialism and technology culture complex. The setting is usually specific locales globally.

What drew the attention of critics to Sonny Okosun was his album "Papa's Land". As soon as he got his continental recognition from that song-text of propaganda, he moved from Africa to the Third World with the same patriotic political jingles. He thus came into spiritual union with superstars like Peter Tosh (himself a colleague of Bob Marley in the original Wailers). From thence he was catapulted into the arena of black musicians fighting apartheid of any kind anywhere. The dailies featured headlines about his second attempt to win American recognition. The dailies' caption of his tours announce "Americans Yield to Okosun's Ozzidism", "Okosun: What the Yankees missed", etc.

Of course, Nigerian musicians have launched what could be tagged as "Operation Reverse Incursion". King Sunny Ade had a word with the Japanese Foreign Minister in Tokyo; Chief Ebenezer Obey has been credited with "Nigeria exports her music" by journalists; Sonny Okosun is making a simultaneous thrust with the power of song-texts. While he is busy propagating from his musical soap-box abroad, he also puts his song-texts into the voices of blind musicians, kids and emerging stars in Nigeria. He discusses the need for a clean environment through a little nine-year-old girl, Yvonne Maha, the daughter of a well-known Nigerian music critic, Phil Maha. Chukwume Ijelonu, an 18 year-old blind boy who possesses a West African School Certificate and has the ambition to be a popular musician, has a text written by Sonny Okosun to sing. Nigeria's emerging female star, Onyeka Onwenu, has already sung Sonny Okosun's "Endless Life" among her innovative mixed packages. They may be called pot pourri - albums comprising foreign top-of-the-chart of yester-years, adaptations of local folk "classics" through which she up-dates works of some Nigerian artists like those of this author and those of late Harcourt

Whyte, the well-known composer of "choral" music, who was also a choirmaster of great reputation. His work has influenced an outstanding number of Nigerian gospel singers and composers just as Patty Obassey admits that this author's song "*Nye Ayi Miri Ndu*" was one of his earliest sources of inspiration. A critic also accepted that this author's song "*Ilu Ndi Igbo*" (1967) -Proverbs of Ndi Igbo must have influenced the lyrical style Ofigbo song-texts and musicians after its release on Phillips (West Africa) Records.

In Africa, urban popular music rhythms are known as "sound" while song-texts are known as "messages". Rhythms which lack song-texts of serious themes are devoid of messages because they are not tied-up with authentic life style of the people, their integrity, their aspirations and their struggle for total independence. Urban popular rhythms on their own, at socializing centres, are left for the party addict, public relations man, the tourist, the frustrated man, the man in search of relaxation, the reveller and the consumer with specific problems socially, psychologically and even medically.

A young journalist once referred to highlife as "fading riding fad". Such limitations in critical appreciation result in Africa's alienation even in spite of significant contributions from Africa. Highlife is undergoing technological evolution and among factors responsible for this progressive change is Sonny Okosun's Ozzidism.

Sonny Okosun was born in Enugu in Nigeria on 1 January, 1947. "The Postmen" was his first showbiz group based at Enugu in 1965. He flirted with the job of a designer for NBC-TV in Lagos, in 1968. He thereafter turned a guitarist in Victor Uwaifo's band. He has participated in many 'International Festivals of the Arts.' He was also cast for "The Cinemas of Ramond Park" or "MAU strike at Dawn" - a film shot in London. Shortly after, his professional band "Paperback Limited" was born which he later rechristened Ozzidism.

The Okosun campaign for a world-wide recognition of African Pop music and his passion for spreading his Pan-African song-texts have begun to concretize. According to a write-up culled from American statesman, Sonny Okosun has begun an "extended plan of conquest:"

> To the best of my knowledge, Nigeria has no extended plan of conquest, yet a small troupe of crack Nigerian troops caused a much larger number of Texas – several hundreds of them, in fact, to surrender within minutes at Liberty lunch Sunday night. Sonny Okosun and his Oziddi slew a packed

club the nice way: with non-stop music that was so rhythmic and powerful that the only sane response was to give in. It helped that they were a lot of Nigerians in attendance who seemed to know some in-jokes that Sonny Okosun and his two madcap players launched during the evening but that only added a spice (*egusi* seed and alligator pepper) to the entertainment.

Sonny Okosun, in his non-militant but Pan-Africanist stance continued to spread the propaganda of Africa's desire to re-occupy her lost territories. In his "Revolution" he eulogizes Nelson Mandela, the "lion from the mountain" and invoking the spirit of departed heroes of the third world, Sonny Okosun advertises: "We want a leader, not a ruler...Africa wants a leader, not a ruler." There is positivism in Sonny Okosun's propaganda which implies the "platter of gold" political dialogue. There is a flavour of non-violence and gospel of peace evident in his discourse, yet there is an overtone of aggression which does not indicate any offensive in the event of a break-down at the dialogue table:

"Notice not the tree, you brethren, but the roots therein."

It was the third week of February, 1980.
"Fela's appointment is at 11:00 p.m," I reminded my host, looking scared.
John looked at his wrist watch, "I've not forgotten the appointment, Sonny. We'll take off at 10.30 p.m."
"Fela is crazy. This quiet time of the night in Lagos is dangerous, Isn't it? To drive all that way from Surulere to Ikeja."
John Chukwu did not look scared. It was not really that Lagos would be quiet but men of the underworld would be probably at large more effectively at the early hours of the morning when I expected the interview to be over. John is almost a Lagosian. Although he is Igbo and his home is Makor in Awgu local government area of Enugu State in Nigeria, he has been resident in Lagos for a long time. He had played the title role of Amadi in Ola Balogun's film, "*Amadi*" which drew its theme from the Nigerian Civil War.
"But you are flying to New York in a few days."
"Oh, I should be in Paris then. How will you make it?"
"Emeka Nwofor will take me," I said.

"And when is the check-in time?"

"10.30 p.m. or thereabout," I replied. I was now giving up because the flight would depart from Ikeja airport at about twelve midnight and Emeka would still drive back to his own Surulere home.

As we drove along, John said: "Fela is alert all the time. Night is his time of greatest action either in his Shrine or at Kalakuta, his residence."

"O.K., you win," I submitted.

To fix the appointment, John and I were his special guests at his 'Shrine' two weeks earlier.

I had known Fela Ransome-Kuti (that was his name) when his Koola Lobitos and highlife jazz were neither understood by Nigerian dance-rhythm party addicts nor even by some "critics" in the early sixties.

We had met at the temporary campus of Ife University at the Nigerian College of Arts, Science and Technology (Nigercol), Ibadan. Dollar Club was run mainly by students of Pharmacy. I was one of their masters of ceremony. Fela and his Koola Lobitos were on the bandstand. I talked to Fela; that was in December, 1963.

He accepted to play on a fee of J40 at Havana Carnival Nite of 1964. I explained that that was the fee for less known bands but I added that there was something strange and revolutionary in his beats. Thus, among the other bands, he would certainly attract his fellowship and fans. "Sigma Club," I went on, "has an ear for tomorrow's sound, but being pragmatic, we honour today's sound for Havana's fans." The population of Havana fans was so dense that "couples" who at any time separated during the carnival, for individual tastes, could only re-unite at 6.30 a.m. or even 7.00 a.m. when the Carnival Nite wound-up.

At the end of the informal negotiation, at the early hours of the morning, marking the close of Dollar Nite activities, Fela said, "Sonny, you're right, man. When I'm understood, the table will turn...That day will come, I assure you...Soon, man. The fee is not yet an issue... position has got to change..."

When I negotiated with Victor Uwaifo, offering the same fee, he was positive that one day he would be the leading band at Havana. It also came to pass, of course.

John Chukwu pulled up at Fela's Ikeja Kalakuta home at 10.55 p.m. and cut off the engine. "Let's stay in the car," I suggested "and knock on the door exactly at 11.00 p.m." Of course, it was funny to talk about knocking on Fela's door. It was always wide open with a beehive of activities by his 'queens' and 'boys'. Anyway, at 11.00 p.m. we made it. His secretary said he was unaware of the appointment, but he rushed upstairs for consultations.

Fela rushed down in his pants: "man, I wanted to put you off. I didn't quit. I believe you were serious, *hai* J.C."

Fela talked for almost all the six hours until we ran out of tapes. He supplemented by offering a tape. He drew my attention to a reference, a book by John Miller Chernoff with the title *African Rhythm and African Sensibility* and pointed out the pages which briefly listed him analytically. I noted the address of the publishers. The one Fela showed me was his complimentary copy. John and I took leave of him at 5.00 a.m.

No one who talks with Fela and who has the patience to "reach his inner-self" can leave him without an awareness of a new contact with "learning," sanity, great spirit, courage, vision, wilful indiscipline, patriotism, Pan-Africanism, charity, chaos, black power and "hubris" or self destructive forces.

At the beginning of this chapter, I asked several questions about Fela Anikulapo Kuti. I am aware that in spite of my having to lead you to authoritative sources for answers, there will be a stalemate. Johnny Nash puts it aptly when he asserted that although he could now see clearly because the rain was gone, that "there are more questions than answers, the more I find out, the less I know..."

Probably, it is best to see part of Fela through two writers and one journalist. John Miller Chernoff sees him as "the great Nigerian musician and composer...inventor of afro-beat who inspires the ladies to dance and then tease them." He observes, "In a more serious vein, because people expect their (a reference to African musicians) 'music' (in the nightclub of African cities) to be made in reference to the social situation, music-making provides an effective way of focusing attention and commenting on issues of social concern and importance..."

Carlos Moore, in his great in-depth work on Fela (Moore's wife, Shawna Moore, even translated an original work in French about Fela from the title *Fela, Fela, cette, puttain de vie*, to *Fela, Fela, this bitch of a life*), has this to say: "this...is not just a biography of a celebrity...then everything about this volcanic music called 'Afro Beat' and the tumultuous, tormented life of its creator speaks to and about the lives, struggle and hopes of hundreds of millions of men and women who, scattered through Mother Africa." Carlos Moore then observes:

> Fela disturbs, annoys, upsets. He personifies controversy. Many love his powerful music but detest Fela the man. Others fascinated by his political and

social discourse, remain more or less insensitive to the magical music enveloping the message. Then there are any number who unhesitatingly reject both the man and his music and who wish he would disappear.

Before Moore let his readers listen to Fela himself, he wonders:

> Where them, does one pin-point the 'critical moment of raw truth, about someone so immensely charismatic that at times even he finds himself hemmed in between the flattering image of his countless fans and the scornful depiction of his detractors...?
> Why all the fuss over this man, who before being a 'Nigerian,' sees himself first as an African?

And, according to Gbenga Ayodele, Fela himself once said:

> ...the government can't touch me. For one thing they think I'm crazy. If I were a respected professor at a University rebelling this way, that would be something different. But then I am just a musician, a crazy artist, saying a lot of crazy things. And then they take a look at what I stand for, nationalism, Pan-Africanism, and anti-colonialism. These are things they say they stand for, so if they come down on me, they would be coming down on themselves.

Gbenga Ayodele concludes:

> Fela is probably the only musician in the world to be charged with armed robbery, sedition and drug addiction, yet he remains the most original force in African music since the World War.

The result of Fela's indiscriminate prejudice against military regimes is his miscalculations as indicated in his assertion above. This time the government "touched" him neatly and legally. He was caught, as the law did, with other Nigerian citizens and foreigners and charged with economic sabotage. Would this lend credibility to Gbenga Ayodele's contradictory tag that "Fela is a rebel without a cause, a

conformist who has made career out of non-conformism?"
He went on:

> Authoritarianism has always appealed to Fela, who despite his sympathies for the under-dog, is in many respects a mirror of the materialistic society he criticizes...

Yet Mr. Ayodele emphasizes,

> "Fela...is not just an artist, he is a philosopher. He is to possibly millions of youths of this country, a lodestar, a subject of admiration, a destroyer of myths, a personification of the quintessence of African culture, the most controversial musician in the country..."

He then highlights the complex personality of Fela when he says:

> Mr. Femi Falana, a lawyer by profession...thinks Fela is the best musician in the country, keeping out prejudices. According to him, it is a pity that most Nigerians still fail to understand the musical philosophy of the Chief priest and recognize him as a responsible adult.

In that near-biographical write-up of the March issue of *Spear*, captioned "Kalakuta without Fela," Mr. Ayodele concludes: "Fela...is the musical conscience of independent Africa."

The two writers above represent foreign opinion about Fela Anikulapo Kuti, while the journalist obviously represents the "home-voice".

Most celebrities are not usually honoured in their life-time, especially if they are stepping on big toes, fearlessly and aggressively. In their lifetime, they also refuse to be identified with selfish motives of the established opposition camp.

It is an established fact that leadership may not necessarily comprise only nationalists and loyalists but then a good proportion of "the opposition" may be retrogressive and power-seeking lackeys who would provide no better alternatives. Even among the "independent party", we may find neutralists who are potential dictators and materialists.

Every working class man is not necessarily a victim of a "Babylon System". The more difficult it becomes for one to properly place who the suffering masses really are in a developing country, the more difficult it becomes to understand the nationalistic and patriotic critics of establishments like Fela Anikulapo-Kuti. Have we not seen many labourers convert to employers and wealthy managing directors overnight and no questions asked by the society? Have we not seen those who owned only push-bikes convert overnight to business tycoons with chauffeurs?

Fela is even aware of his major weakness, and that is his inability to apply the break at the right moment. Of course, the illiterate population in Africa is also reflected by the fickleness of acceptance and rejection, fanaticism and hard-line prejudices. Then, there is the third factor: the history of Fela's genealogical tree, as well as Fela's background as a child and youth, which must first be understood, as did Carlos Moore, before the mysteries surrounding Fela's "messiahship" can be impartially assessed.

Why do his countrymen think he is not a responsible adult? They think Fela is building himself up as an outlaw and no nation would tolerate an outlaw. They think he is lecherous. He says "Sex is Life". He married twenty-seven wives on 20 February, 1978 to supplement the senior wife. The number of wives decreased: first fifteen loyalists; then down to eight only. Probably, it may revert to his original monogamous number. His countrymen think that he is a "corrupter of youths". That may well be the justifiable opinion of most parents of his wives. Even the fans, including the old and the young, who heralded Fela's entry into the "opposition camp" have decamped considerably.

Fela Anikulapo-Kuti threatened to become a politician, but he gave it up to his lawyer, who himself was also interested in the presidency. They had discussed and decided to work together. Fela pointed out: "I was ready to let him run for presidency in my place. Really, I don't want to be president, you know. Once the ideas I am fighting for are there, I don't need to be president...Then on another day I went to see him to discuss the situation of poor people and ideas, not just on bettering the lot of people but changing it..."

I consider Carlos Moore as a commendable authority now on Fela's biography (also along with the French original Shawna Moore translated). It is therefore important to re-emphasize, in a most abridged form, a very few selected and relevant background from Moore's work aimed at amplifying the paradoxes of Fela's militarism even in his sex life.

In Fela's mother's description (Funmilayo) Moore's paints the verbal picture of a woman marked by destiny: "She was to stir up Abeokuta; strike fear in the hearts of those serving the British rulers; become a pioneer of the fight for the independence of Nigeria; ignite the fire of the women's rights and struggle in Africa and beget a rebel."

Fela, according to Moore, claims that he is an *abiku* because a *babalawo* confirmed that he was first born in 1935; because his father, the Right Reverend Israel Oludotun Ransome-Kuti, was an overzealous Christian, he discarded the Yoruba naming culture. So Fela, was named Hildegart by a German missionary. For these reasons the "first Fela" died. The second Fela was born, after three years, in 1938 and culturally named Fela. Fela himself then added:

> Hildegart!...Hildegart...Me, who was supposed to come and talk about Blackism and Africanism, the plight of my people...I felt that name like a wound...Bear the name of the conquerors...? Two weeks after my first birth, my soul left my body for the world of the spirits.

A *babalawo* had already prophesied that Fela "will be stubborn...His wives will be numerous...He will flaunt laws...will live in poverty alongside beggars and thieves..."

Fela passed through a crucible of uncompromising discipline as a child and even during his early youth. He recalls nostalgically "between my mother and father combined, I got three thousand strokes between the ages of nine and seventeen." Fela, at nineteen (even when he was now in London studying classical music in Trinity College of Music was scared of women, drinking and smoking because of his fanatical religious upbringing. J. K. Braimah, Fela's true friend, who actually started 'Koola Lobitos' with him in London, confirmed this in an interview with Carlos Moore. How many of his countrymen know this much about Fela Anikulapo-Kuti?

Fela's father clashed with the colonial military authorities in his own time and caused the military post to be removed from the heart of Abeokuta to the outskirts of the city. He also "flogged" a British colonial education officer who insisted on inspecting Abeokuta Grammar School founded and owned by him - Right Reverend Israel O. Ransome Kuti. Fela's mother boldly told off a young British District Officer at Abeokuta whom she considered insulting: "...you bastard, rude little rat." *The Daily News* of late forties would confirm that. The self-exile of the *Alake* of Abeokuta to Oshogbo for nearly three years, would also confirm the militarism of Fela's mother as well as the seizure of her passport during Sir Tafawa Balewa's first phase as Prime Minister in the colonial government. Why? Fela's mother made unauthorized tour of the "Iron Curtain" countries of the world.

The complementary nature of the sound of music and song-texts are more manifest in the examples of the works of the three musicians examined in this chapter. Their works also concretise the growth and the role of music within a national triangular framework: culturally, socially and politically; and in this context, economic growth is an appendage of national political maturity. Israel Nwoba's lyric was a harmless mirror which projected our social inadequacies lightly. Sonny Okosun's Ozzidism has been accelerating its fire on his efforts to alert us about the new plague of "neo-negrophobism" and the need for solidarity at the home-front. Fela Anikulapo-Kuti has, in many ways, challenged Africans spiritually, culturally, socially, economically and politically in order to enable us see the path in the Red Sea for a reunion with ourselves. At the other end, beyond the Red Sea, he has a vision of the old Africa reasserting her leadership position.

The forward march is on, but we still ask "who made thee judge over us?" And were not the two, both Israelites and the kinsmen of Moses, the authors of the same question and suspicion, respectively?

# 3

# E.T. Mensah and Ghana's Repertory

A critic had observed that "the history of Ghanaian music cannot be complete without including the evolvement of our highlife music and those who helped to originate it." He described E.T. Mensah as "the King of Highlife".

E.T. Mensah himself confirms that the title is not one of those indiscriminate ones flung at heroes by their fans. He leads us into the truth. He says that "although he had been using the title previously as a publicity gimmick, it was officially conferred on him in 1957 by the Arts Council of Ghana in appreciation of the way he had developed the music. He was given a native stool as the symbol of his kingship." E.T. then says "he has no abdication plans even though age is catching up fast on him." He concluded: "When I pass off they can elect another king to step into my throne."

He also convincingly settled the irrelevant conflict involving musicians and critics, over the years, about who really introduced highlife to the West Coast of Africa.

The fact that E.T. Mensah's assertion, made in 1984, took place on Nigerian soil in the presence of Nigeria's Victor Olaiya, is significant.

Dr. Victor Olaiya confirms that he is an uncrowned king of highlife. He was usually referred to as the "Evil Genius of Highlife". He recalled the early years of Sigma Club's "Havana music festival of the University of Ibadan. It was a title invented by either the press or the undergraduates of University of Ibadan during the Havana."

Ghana's repertory of highlife dance bands date back to early forties when they usually had what was called "Jam sessions". 1947 was the year E.T. Mensah resigned from government service as a pharmacist and opted for a career in music.

Ghana indisputably remains a homeland of popular highlife dance bands. In this chapter you are brought into contact with some Ghanaian highlife musicians whose contributions enhanced the "introduction and development of African musical idiom in the area of highlife."

## K. Gyasi
*K. Gyasi and His Noble Kings*

> The statement that highlife originated from Ghana has been debated by many people, but 1 am fully convinced that Ghana can rightfully claim to a large extent to the progenitor of this up-beat music which is rooted in the spontaneous, moonlit get-together of traditional Ghana music which was originally known by the indigenous name "OSIBI". Attempts to revert from the highlife to Osibi have failed - so we are stuck with Highlife, which is a corrupt name given to "OUR" music by the early colonialist who had the desire to dance to our music.
>
> *- Mike Eghan, The Emperor*

Mike Eghan, The Emperor argues that "as a result, the name "highlife" has become a vast umbrella covering a variety of our traditional music. However, many of our musicians have worked hard over the years to maintain the warmth and rhythms and social commentary of the highlife."

This is where I switch the spotlight onto Dr. K. Gyasi for however short the list of those who contributed to highlife music in Ghana, K. Gyasi's name comes within the top bracket - a fact which underscores the reason why he has been dubbed the 'HIGH-LIFE DOCTOR.'

"Dr. K. Gyasi, I don't mean to drop names, but Dr. K. Gyasi's name is and will always be one of the best attention-getters because of his immense contribution to highlife music."

> As a guitarist, composer and singer, Dr. K. Gyasi has a number of 'FIRSTS' to his credit. He is first and foremost one of the pioneers in our local guitar band music. He is the first man to introduce the sound of electronic organ into guitar band music in Ghana.

Again, he is the first to add Blowing - or Wind - instruments effectively to his band, an example which is being followed by other groups in the country today."

"One of his best hits is 'Sikyi-highlife.' "Sikyi" is one of the several down-to-earth forms of our traditional songs, rhythms and dances. Like most of our past times, Sikyi is performed on moonlit nights by the exuberant youth. They sing about events of the day, love and hate, hunger and poverty, happiness and sadness and through the rhythms and melodies, render social commentary."

## E. K. Nyame
*(Founder of E. K.'s Band of Ghana)*

"In fact, I was the man who first made a conscious attempt to project the 'highlife' music as it is today by guitar bands."

Kwasi Ampadu-Boateng writes about the great works of E. M. Nyame. In "Sankofa" (Go Back And Retrieve), Mr. Ampadu-Boateng presents the Ghanaian musician who became so popular that it was enough to mention just his initials: E. K.

Mr. Ampadu-Boateng observes:

"It is not easy to hit the top of the chart with a maiden release, but this the E.K's Band did with amazing ease. And this I think goes to justify their claim of being the greatest Guitar Band of all time. For in 1951, when their first song "Small Boy Nye Me Eia" appeared on Decca WA 001, there was a spontaneous scramble for it. Every lover of good music struggled to have one secured in his custody. Thanks to the foresight and financial support of an expatriate music lover, H. Teymani Hammoud. It was he who purchased instruments for the budding group that was to dominate the guitar band scene for a complete decade.

The imposing musical personality of the great Sam, composer of the evergreen "*Ya Amponsah*" had left the platform by the beginning of the 1950s. The vacuum created was so great. In fact, the then Gold Coast was yearning for a successor. Then E.K. Nyame and Kobinakai, both formerly with Appiah Agyekum's Band emerged. They came together in 1950, performing mainly at parties for the *nouveau riche* and sometimes when the going was tough, they pitched their camp somewhere in town to collect pennies. During one of such outings, Mr. Edwards saw them. He at once found in them the qualities of good musicians and decided wisely to organize them into a group capable of putting songs onto wax for commercialization. That was the beginning of greater things to come and up till now, the name E.K's Band readily brings back memories of the glorious years of the guitar band reign.

Of course, there were other personalities that helped to produce the unique sounds of the E. K's Band -Paa Kwesi, Willie, S.K. Appiah and Kwesi Plange just to mention a few, worked so closely together that the band was unquestionably the nation's number one. No wonder they had the privilege of accompanying the late President Dr. Kwame Nkrumah to Liberia at the invitation of the late President William Taubman. That was really a great honour befitting a great band and that's why today they stand, enveloped in pride, looking back at their own achievements. Dan Chie Awere, who goes by the Showbiz name 'Ride Away' has spent sleepless nights and trekked many miles conducting a survey to know which of the many hits of E. K.'s Band that music lovers will want to hear again. Mr, Ampadu-Boateng describes Awere as a young man of "hard work and dynamism".

## Jerry Hansen
*And The Ramblers Dance Band*

> It is a decade now since Decca began recording local artists in West Africa. During this stretch of time Dance Bands have sprouted, flowered and wilted away to die in the true tradition of musical groups. Somehow, one band seemed to have stayed around longer than most; it seems to have succeeded where others failed. The Ramblers Dance Band, nearly eight years old has introduced glamour into the West African Highlife Scene.
> 
> *- Frank Hayfron (1969)*

As at the time Frank Hayfron did this write-up, "The Ramblers Dance Band" comprised Ferdinand Asere and Lawrence Osafo (Trumpets); Jerry Hansen and Felix Amenuano (Tenor Saxophone);

Arthur Plange and Patrick Forson (Alto Saxophone); Felix Amenuano and Ferdinand Asare (Flutes); Frank Croffie (Guitar); Eddie Soga (Bass); Eddie Owoo (Drums); Nat Fleischer (Conga); Nee Quaye (Maracas) and Joe Archiso and Charles Kojo were vocalists.

Jerry Hansen was one of the Ghanaian musicians who saw Efik, a Nigerian language, as a language of music. "*Ekombi*" and "*Ima Abasi*" were two song-texts in Efik which lingered nostalgically.

Frank Hayfron included them among what he described as "sensational hits". He continues:

> ...thirteen tracks of the finest arrangements of highlife ever produced. Eight of the tunes were penned by three of Ghana's most talented pop composer; two are Ewe songs of anonymous composers; another two are by a Nigerian composer, Len Bassey and the thirteenth is by a Black American singer.

Mr. Hayfron then comments on the tracks:

> "Ekombi" whose rhythm, the Akwete, is a Nigerian addition to the highlife presents a Conga solo which for its very African touch is simply exhilarating. Frank Croffle's guitar solo in "Agyanka Dabre" manages to convey to the listener the lonely state of the orphan. "Ama Bonsu" introduces two wooden flutes (which are native and are played like trumpets, i.e. with the axis perpendicular to the line of the mouth) and Jerry Hensen lends it a lot of depth when he interrupts these flutes and a muted trumpet with hill tenor saxophone. "*Nyame Ne Nhyehyeɛ*" has a powerful introduction and the authors influence is noticed in "*Nyame Mberɛ*" where very fine flute work is provided. "*Alome,*" which is one of the traditional Ewe tunes...changes its beat halfway into the Agbaza, and Ewe dance.
>
> "Knock on Wood," with English lyrics has been around as a "Soul" number ... "*Onua Pa Due*" brings a third singer into the act ... settles into a slow highlife for voices, guitar and percussion. "*Ima Abasi*" is another Akwete from Nigeria and "Better Ni" is highlife with a strong jazz influence. "*Gyae Su Na Nkomi Dǎ*" is beauty but short and "*Meda Ebefa*" has a nice steady rhythm and the flute accompaniment is rather

attractive. "*Meni Nda Obiara Sɔ*" is further justification of the Band's claim to being the finest in West Africa. Jerry Hansen's material is given a very slow but neat treatment and Eddie Soga on the base is particularly delightful. The duet vocal technique employed by this band has been very successful.

Mr. Hayfron concludes:

That highlife is West Africa's own beat. It is older than the "Soul" or the "Twist" and even the "Rock and Roll;" it will still be around when we leave. Whether in European suits or our own Kente cloths,"Joromis" or"Danshikes," we will still manage to keep the happy grins on our faces as we sway on the dance floor...

# Ralph Adusah
*Leader of Abibifa Dance Band of Ghana*

Ralph Adusah was born at Kibi, the capital of Akin Abuakwa, Eastern Region, Ghana. He attended the Presbyterian High School there and completed his studies there in 1965.

Mr. Adusah apprenticed himself to one Mr. Adjei, a retired performing musician for the art of guitar playing. Mr. Adjei, at that time, was a worker at Kibi in 1966.

Ralph played with three top groups in Kumasi, namely: The Ambassadors, The Afro Beats and Dr. K. Gyasi's Noble Kings in the Ashanti capital from 1968-1973. The last group he played with in Kumasi was that of K. Gyasi's.

Ralph learnt the art of composition and song writing under the "Highlife Doctor" - K. Gyasi.

He left Kumasi for Tema where he played with the Food Complex Corporation Band (The Complex Sounds) between 1974 and 1975. He later left "The Sounds" to form "The Abibifo Band of Ghana". "Abibifo" or "The Black Race" is a band with a very good outfit. It is a twenty-one man band that has got the highlife music at a very tentative angle to display. The band's music has got all it takes to go places. The blending of the guitar with horns and the crescendos of drums and congas with the harmonious vocals calls the attention of the listener.

The Abibifo is a unique band with all to offer. It is a band that will keep the people alive with highlife beats for a long time to come.

## Party Time with "CEEKAY"

Not too long ago, C.K. Mann expected his admirers to study and catch up to be able to appreciate his kind of music effectively-conditioning, so to speak. Now, 1 suspect he is satisfied, if not elated to move enthusiastic fans by the sheer emotional impact of his music. Essentially, his achievement is due to a high original mind, one that looks acutely at every tune from a distinctively personal view-point.

"Mann" is a man strongly built, of the qualities of a light-heavy weight boxer, medium height and dark in complexion, he projects his strength in strumming the guitar. Being fascinated by South America's captivating rhythms during one of his trips to that continent as a seaman, he there and then decided to become a musician with preference to the guitar as his medium of expression.

After sometime with Kakaiku's Guitar Band of Ghana in which group he served his apprenticeship in guitar playing, (C.K. as he is popularly known in Ghana) then joined the "Ocean Strings" which he led till 1966. The band folded up and a benefactor, Mr. Anis Moubaratk, proprietor of Princess Cinema, came to the rescue. He had known C. K. who used to 'jam' at the "Princess" now and then. Anis had the instruments and the night spot and so invited C. K. to lead the newly formed "Carousel 7" as resident band of the "Princess" night club, "Carousel Ago-go" Takoradi. He then came to prominence with a single hit record "*Edina Benya*" in 1969.

This has been of course followed by unprecedented string of top sellers that have made C.K. Mann a giant figure in the Ghanaian music zone. C.K. Mann's guitar playing is full of measures of swinging propulsiveness. He has complete independence of expression on the guitar. In projecting his inner self when soloing, he directs his hands to execute marvels on the guitars whether employing single strings of block chordial work. Kofi does not only play the guitar, but also sings. Here, special mention must be made of how, when singing he lets the lyrics roll off his tongue like "Soft Smooth Grapes". He possesses an individualistic vocal tremulous, and that is prominent of his work out in "*M'atow Abo Wa*" an authentic wailer, characteristic of the Africa.

Blending authentic African rhythms and complete European structures, Mr. Mann produces what is typical of his own creation. His rhythmic prowess and harmonic sense are eminent in "*Medze Me Ho*

*Bema Nyame No Som Pa"* (I shall dedicate myself with good service to the Lord) a form conveniently symbolized as A—B—A.

"Hats off to his cohorts, who helped to bring his show to the pinnacle of his music career." They have developed a music comradeship which is very inventive and delightful. They infuse into every tune a criss-cross of ideas, a constant interchange of rhythmic concepts and coloration which require an overwhelming musician-ship.

The chart-bursting record *"Nimpa Rebre"* sang by Pat Thomas and Kofi Yankwon in a memorable duet work which earned C.K. the coveted total "King of Highlife" in 1971.

The first side of this record offers listeners a whole lot of 27 minutes non-stop melody of OSODE tunes. This is probably the longest side of any record, and must be a bonus from "Essiebons".

## Joe Mensah

Fans who could remember the good old days in the early sixties at the Ambassador Hotel, Yaba, Lagos, Nigeria will be happy to have an extended work on *"Bonsue,"* *"Rakpokpo"* and *"Bere bere"*. My new compositions are my dedication and respect for the people of Nigeria. *"Ye Gbawa oo Baba"* is composed in the Yoruba language. I seize this opportunity to express my thanks to all the fans for their goodness. I hope that, by the grace of God, my fans and I can continue to enjoy this cordial relationship that has long existed between us. Thanks to all of you. I thank Chief Commander Ebenezer Obey. It all started at the Ambassador Hotel in Yaba, Lagos, Nigeria. The nostalgic memories of millions of my fellow teenagers, whose most enthusiastic idolization and encouragement initiated me fully into showbiz, a few years ago. This initial ideation was the most concrete foundation that has kept me up till today, as a renowned African singer, musician, composer and band leader. The memories of these millions of loving and sincerely affectionate fans have been the miraculous panacea for me against any kinds of ills or upsets or hardships in showbiz, especially while in the USA. From the Ambassador Hotel, Yaba, Lagos, during an almost religious event on every Sunday, called "tea time dance" to the arenas and every stage I have mounted, I shall always be saying "thank you" to everyone, each time I mount a stage.

Till eternity, I thank you immensely. My record is for you my fans, old, new and yet to come. But, especially, to those who are gone before us, some government leaders, some governors, some society elite, some business executives, some professional men, some just humble and poor, some still struggling to find place, some in whatever situation, wherever they are, I made this record for you. My adorable and most cherished memories, and a most honourable dedication to the late great Chief Bill Friday. May his best days, his life and the many tones of happiness be brought, through his trumpet, to so many people be forever remembered.

## Highlife in Ghana: the Pace-Setters
*by E. Quarcoo and Abu Abarry-Ali, (both Ghanaians)*

Scholars see highlife musicians of Ghana as pacesetters. The study below is reproduced to establish their contributions.

Akwasi Sanpong (1974) gives a brief survey of traditional music in Ghana. He notes that drums, flutes, horns, gongs and rattles appear to be the most common musical instruments used in traditional music all over Ghana. These instruments can be played alone or in combination with other instruments, with the appropriate vocal accompaniment to put across the required rhythm and verbal message during traditional festivals.

It used to be argued among scholars that philosophies are the preserves of Europe, America, their kinsmen the world over and the East; that Africans did not seem to have any philosophical leanings. This mistaken conception came from the wrong assumption that even though Africans verbalize a lot; no instances of prolonged argumentation about life occur among them. That wrong assumption can be debunked by merely examining some of the themes of the songs that Africans sing; the symbolism of the musical instruments they use and the messages they communicate through their songs. Through his song, the Ghanaian, for example, praises heroes and groups for outstanding achievements; this eulogy is extended to those who have traditionally defended the society successfully at war and organized people in self-help activities, etc. The Ghanaian musician also praises the chief, if he is hard-working and fatherly. Songs in Ghanaian traditional society are also used to abuse those who deserve the scorn of society for various kinds of immoral acts and deviant behaviour. When in lighter moods, Ghanaians make songs to create a romantic atmosphere and sing about love and sex. They also complain about domestic and other issues. These songs are sometimes satirical, using idioms and parables. Ghanaian music is equally used to thank those who have been benevolent to society in general, or to their clans. Occasionally, Ghanaian songs are made to ask for favours, or to express satisfaction or disappointment. During naming ceremonies, songs of rejoicings are made. In times of death, dirges are sung or recited for the deceased.

On all these occasions, songs are made and presented by individuals or groups. But the important thing to note is that there exist travelling or mobile bands which go round to perform on festive occasions. These bands may be *ad hoc,* and in the words of Nketsia, the groups are ensemble "of musicians in associative relationship, organized for the making of music and remaining so for as long as the particular form of music they make is popularly supported or patronized."

Ghanaian highlife bands appear to have developed from this travelling and *ad hoc* traditions and each high-life band based on the conclusions above stays on the scene as long as they enjoy the social support they need to sustain them. Highlife bands thus sprang from traditional roots sharing the same messages, orientation, manner of presentation, the same stage or venue orchestration; and audiences basically change with the influence of changing times. The early highlife bands appear to appeal mainly to urbanized and politicized members of society.

It is interesting to note that Ghanaian highlife as result, has for a long time, been an instrument of political mobilization since modern politics reared its head on the social scene of Ghana. Although modem politics appears to aim at capturing the minds of rural Ghanaians, its target seems to be the urban dwellers. Therefore, in the battle-drawn days of political agitation in Ghana, the leaders of highlife music in Ghana E. K. Nyame and his renowned vocalist, Kobinakai, used the lyrics of their music to comment and analyse political and social events of the day. The dominant language for socio-political highlife themes and agitation through highlife music was Akan; and the pace-setters exploited it. They sometimes used English, if they so wished, to address the colonial administration. So, when in 1963 they wanted the Queen of England to feel welcome to Ghana, a song was made for her in the rhythm of highlife "Welcome, welcome, welcome to Ghana..." Political heroes like Nkrumah were immortalized, through highlife, for their wisdom in delivering Ghana from colonialism "*Ataa Obemma Kwame Nkrumah na onimi main, Akwaaba.*"

Apart from these two pioneers, Nyameh and Kobinakai, there is the legendary E. T. Mensah who appears to tower over most of the Ghanaian highlife practitioners. E. T. Mensah has been very much popular with his Tempos Band; but highlife historians even say that Tempos Band was not his first band. A pharmacist by profession, a civil servant for that matter, music was more of a hobby to him than a vocation. As leader of the Tempos Band, he developed an expertise with the trumpet, a musical instrument which was then very new on the musical orchestral kit in Ghana.

His songs were mainly in the Ga language and most of it was about love and entertainment. There used to be the time when everybody would like to see E. T. and his band play; and this yearning was not lost upon his ego. He had a highlife number made for this. In that number, the vocalist, playing the role of an E. T. Mensah fan, insisted on accompanying a friend or his lover to see "Gentle E. T. and his group". One of his popular songs, in the 50s, was "*Tsoo Ohami lai momo*" (i.e. shine for me, my old flame). Every liquor-selling bar in Accra had it as a popular number for their customers. The one that swept across the West Coast of Africa "Everybody likes Saturday Night" was the number that really made the Tempos Band.

Meanwhile, among the Akans was a band known as 'African Brothers' led by Ampadu. This band was a bit different in its approach from the E. T. Mensah's and King Bruce's teams. "King Bruce," a Permanent Secretary in the civil service in Accra founded Black Beats Band, which was a contemporary of E. T. Mensah's. One thing significant about them is that the civil servants' bands were careful of the political undertones of the lyrics of their songs whereas the rest of the highlife bands did not care whose ox was gored. The important thing for them was to carry their philosophical messages through to their audiences; and that was exactly what Ampadu did. His question has been "What is life if one is to die soon?" Why do young people die? Why is man a debased creature?"

It is important to note that Ampadu's highlife numbers went down well with the Ghanaian public in moments of crisis. At times, he sounded rather prophetic in terms of expressing people's attitudes and gloom to-wards government inflicted social suffering and consequent yearning of the people for a political change. Some of his memorable numbers of the early sixties were songs with animal characters drawn from fables. In one of them, the main thrust of the message was that the political system was breeding inequality and bullying. In the song, the lyrics, satirized. All the animals were said to have gone to a meeting; during the proceedings, one of the weaker animals, which was sitting near the bear was not given any room by the bear; enough room even to smile when a joke was cracked. Any attempt for the poor animal to assert itself was met with a severe warning, through stamping on its tail by the aggressive and bullying bear. Finally, the oppressed animal gathered all the courage it could muster and exclaimed "petition, please! Point of order." Following this, she was granted the floor. She went to complain that at the meeting where they were all assembled, some animals felt comfortable, while others were not allowed to be so privileged. This became the swan-song of many opponents of Nkrumah and of those who felt oppressed in the society. Tyranny and oppression in offices and work places became a target of attack.

The number so caught up with emotional reactions in Ghana that the African Brothers Band became the "unelected" champions of human rights for the down-trodden. There is no way one could write the history of highlife in Ghana without mentioning these songs and their messages. Almost all their numbers were also in Akan. Some of their numbers were used by coup-makers to herald new governments they wished to establish, if the coup succeeded. To be political is to be controversial, so musicians had some of their numbers that were to have been used in aborted coups, banned. Others were banned because the succeeding governments did not like the messages of their songs. They were too populist and capable of raking open old wounds.

It is necessary to point out that, apart from the highlife of African Brothers, highlife bands which had songs like "the wind precedes the rain" and "I told you and you didn't listen", etc., also had their brushes with the politicians in power in the early sixties. Alongside Ampadu was a policeman, Aunie Johnson (who had rather entertaining numbers on Angelina, Brode kokoo).

This short essay may not be the forum to treat all highlife philosophers of Ghana, but Dr. K. Gyasi and his reliance on traditional rhythm, instruments, myth and folktale cannot be overlooked. He was based in Kumasi and radiated everything that is traditional, blended with the modern. Highlife came from that city; he gave himself a doctorate for his artistry and the idiom of the Akans. Highlife fans enjoy his music wherever his band plays. Thus, because he had a lot to his credit, Dr. K. Gyasi cannot just be brushed aside in the ethnography of music in Ghana.

Moving down South of Ghana, towards the West Coast, one cannot forget Kakaiku and hill guitar band. His was entertainment and relationship with the people. He was the father of most of the highlife leaders of today, including Jerry Hansen. His "*Obiara bet, dama dama*" was the very number recently on Ghana Television; the whole nation went on her feet dancing with him. Unlike the highlife kings mentioned earlier, Kakaiku cannot speak English. He hails from Tarkara, a mining town, with Takoradi as his base; almost all his songs are in Fante and they are mainly for entertainment, pure and simple. One of the boys Kakaiku trained is C.K. Mann, who has become a legend himself in modem Osode music.

C. K. Mann is a farm boy from Elmira, who started his career in the Ghana Navy. Instead of staying on there to become a commodore, he left the navy but could not leave the navy town of Takoradi. He joined a band in Takoradi and later formed his own band named "The Carousel 7". The band rocked the whole of western and central regions of Ghana in the late sixties and early seventies with its Osode music. Some of the memorable numbers they made include *Maame Wokayese nyimpa bebre* - i.e. "Mother, you warned that man would suffer". The story, almost legendary, was that children who would not submit to parental guidance in their youthful days suffer later an in life. This admonishing is confirmed by the words of this song and at the time it was released, it was a hit overnight. C.K. Mann has many other songs, most of which have been compiled in the album "*Party Time*".

The highlife music scene of Ghana has been very fertile. Quite a number of bands and band leaders have come and gone. It is not a male-dominated field. There are such females as Charlotte Dada and lately, Afua Agyepong. Some sing pure highlife, while others add gospel music to their highlife numbers; also the field in Ghana has not been dominated by Ghanaians alone. One name that cannot be brushed aside, when talking about highlife in Ghana, is that of Bob Cole. This very entertaining Nigerian, who grew up in Fanteland, has quite a number of songs to his credit. A memorable highlife number of his is '*Abankaba*'. He doesn't believe that if a home is run well, children can become delinquents. It is children from bad homes who are usually shackled with handcuffs. That is the message of '*Abankaba*'. One can just imagine how parents would rejoice in such a number with a moral to teach. When he first visited Nigeria in the sixties, he recorded his experiences later in a very funny number in Ghana. What he succeeded in doing was to introduce his admirers to some of the names of Nigerian cities which his Ghanaian admirers did not know of before. His experiences did not seem very encouraging, so he didn't make another visit to his own country.

Well, the field of highlife in Ghana is broad. New instruments are introduced every now and then. Once in a while, western music tries to overthrow highlife but, as the name implies, highlife is high and resilient. It has stayed on for decades and may very well survive a century. Many names of bands and artistes have been left out in this short essay. This is because we cannot talk about everybody at the same time. Names of instruments and some styles of highlife have also been left out. This is because we are not writing about instruments *per se* in this essay. All these omissions should form the basis of further research. The field is fertile and the challenges are many.

# 4

# Blowing their own trumpets

We will open this chapter with the background of a Nigerian broadcasting celebrity, Mike Enahoro, whose experience is of great significance to the theme of this study. Until Bobby Benson changed the status of musicians by industrializing popular music, the Nigerian musician was associated with the dregs of the society. He was also tagged an academic drop-out if he had the opportunity of attempting to acquire Western education. It was assumed that he lived a reckless and irresponsible life as an alcoholic, a drug-addict, a pimp, a pauper, a prodigal and a homeless man with an embarrassing family background.

Given the prejudices of the society, reviewers concerned themselves with the musicians' African rhythms only, whereas under such circumstances, a cull from the *curriculum vitae* of the musicians should have been considered vital to the reviews of their works because their family ego was at stake. In spite of the fact that before entertainment became an industry, which produced wealthy superstars, unpatronized artists were socially underrated; local indigenous reviewers themselves should have paved the way for a critical assessment of the artist and his works. This would have brought about an unbiased evaluation of the respectable functional roles of the musicians within the society.

Let us look at a sample of the list of performing artists of the popular music -highlife, from the early fifties. It includes Sammy Akpabot, who tapped his own talents in music even when he was studying at King's College in Lagos (He is currently a well-established scholar and professor of music); Bala Miller, who was top executive of some commercial firms -he is of clerical parentage, being the son of a chaplain of Christ Church Cathedral in Lagos; Mike Enahoro, who did not mind "the threat of excommunication" implied in the reaction of his aristocratic father (He had made up his mind to stay put in "showbiz" by climbing towards the heights through a career in music. Fela Anikulapo-Kuti's mother was among the pioneering nationalists and politicians responsible for the achievement of political independence for Nigeria; Fela's father ranked high in ecclesiastical hierarchy.

Victor Uwaifo went to school at one of Nigeria's "ivy" grammar schools. Zeal Onyia had western professional music credentials and an educator as a parent. The scholarly gentleman of Nigerian country music,

Bongos Ikwue, gave up his university studies in Electrical Engineering for a career in music, drawing from the broad roots of African highlife rhythms. Art Alade stood astride jazz, highlife and showbiz. In Ghana, the picture is the same: E.T. Mensah, Sammy Lartey, Jerry Hansen, Stan Plange and others with respectable professional and academic backgrounds.

Background could be relevant to visions, operations and even achievements. Because of the degree of literacy level in Nigeria, it was easy for the jaundiced views of a small group to influence a majority opinion. For instance, Fela Anikulapo-Kuti, aware that for any revolution to succeed, the follower-ship of youths was important, launched his musical campaign to rally them. No sooner did his strategy of capturing the future decision and policy-makers gather momentum and began yielding results, than he was attacked with a missile of character assassination. He was branded an "Indian hemp smoker," "a non-conformist," "a corrupter of youths," "irresponsible and mad offspring of a respected family" and "a pagan-prodigal son of a respected clergyman." These innuendos are natural taunts and tags associated with "pioneer-ship." If Fela became a head of state, his critics would revert to sycophancy and eulogies. Even when revolutionaries are in power, they are greeted with the same disloyal hypocrisy responsible for the downfall of corrupt powers, and as a Yoruba wit put it, "The tongue is a bad thing... a counsellor uses his tongue to give a bad advice to the Oba." Of course, the wit, according to Harold Courlander, in his book entitled *Tales of Yoruba Gods and Heroes,* was proving that the tongue was capable of offering the best and the worst.

Between the fifties and the eighties the noticeable growth of highlife music was not only astronomical but also became so tied up with purgation, peace and stability that fanaticism for sweet rhythms became a far cry from the innovative ixionic demands of contemporary patterns, in which every shift in rhythm was an index of new dimensions in ideas. As far as we are aware, we are now on the fourth gear in the rhythms of highlife: Jazz-highlife, Ballad-highlife, Ozzidihighlife, and Afro-beat-highlife. Within Afro-beat, there is an intricate gear system producing new dimensions.

Highlife musicians are now guided by a recognizable clarity in their visions, philosophies and goals. For instance, we are aware of the cultural and political stance of Fela Anikulapo-Kuti. Fela is identified as a politician in music. He had intended to run for the office of Presidency of the Federal Republic of Nigeria but his political party which Mr. Bolaji Ademusu recalled as "Young African Pioneers (YAP)" later publicized as "Movement of the People (MOP)" was laid to rest.

Bala Miller has settled for developing musicians, by operating his recommendations that "novitiates" in music need a formal professional and academic exposure, at least enough to lift them from depending solely on their own talents.

Mike Ejeagha has over three hundred materials recorded on tapes resulting from his field work in Igbo folklore highlife music. Mr. Ejeagha, on his own initiative, deposited these materials in the Nigerian National Archives as facilities for researchers (and mark you, Mike Ejeagha is not a product of the ivory tower or its equivalents). This makes his contribution towards knowledge very significant.

Victor Uwaifo is happy that his contribution in the development of highlife music has become a subject of scholarly study at the University of Ilorin in Nigeria.

Before Inyang Henshaw died, he became an instructor or "Arts Fellow" at the University of Calabar's Department of Theatre Arts.

The more we get to know the struggles and sufferings, stresses and strains, contempt and heroes' fanfare and rise, downfall and fluctuating fortunes of African highlife musicians, the closer we will be to artists who in their life-time, joined their more advantaged counterparts in developed countries to design and erect their own monuments towards the enrichment of world history.

Before Bobby Benson, a Nigerian performing musician had no option in employment opportunities. Benson's main employer was a foreign hotel industry businessman not committed to the wave of patriotism and nationalism in Nigeria. His business included the running of night-clubs and brothels in order to maximize his income and returns with fees accruing from lodgings which accommodated prostitutes. The Nigerian performing musician, as his employee, became his victim.

The musician was thus exposed to contamination with the presence of harlots and men of the underworld. He was also open to regular insults from his employer in spite of the fact that his boss was busy looting the wealth of his homeland. It was usual for such employers to acquire Nigerian citizenship, like their kith and kin in other parts of Africa, in order to continue pirating Nigerian foreign exchange (or partly British colonial foreign exchange) for the benefit of their home countries.

The musician was under-paid by his employer and thus underrated by his own age-mates who were farmers and petty traders back in the village or "white-collar job" employees in the townships. These disadvantages inevitably generated a protective attitude by "privileged" Nigerian families and parentage. Since they treated the musician's career with contempt, they prevented their wards from becoming performing musicians.

This parental protective attitude was not a hangover from the universal Roman attitude whereby the profession of arts was left for slaves in contrast to Greek classical concept and practice of the arts; nor was it generally part of the "war" between classical professional disciplines and the arts (in spite of identifiable evidence of collaboration in some cases); but it was an exercise of Nigerian traditional propriety in domestic responsibility.

By far the greatest personal frustrations which performing musicians experienced, after the early years of struggle and poverty, were those connected with public reaction and recognition; lack of supportive funding (since there were no national social security schemes); as well as suspicion between them and recording companies in terms of royalty based on integrity. There was also a dearth of agency institutions which would act as intermediaries for the welfare and rights of the performing musicians.

It is a well-established fact that recording companies never take initiatives to improve the earning powers of musicians. Occasional "Promoters," even if they are indigenes, dictate the kind of rhythms currently in demand in the West. That was why a foreign company in Lagos lost Prince Nico Mgbarga's "Sweet Mother" (which later became a "world classic") to an indigenous entrepreneur with limited financial resources for the effective distribution of "Sweet Mother" beyond Nigeria. That indigenous company at Onitsha, in Nigeria, did come to the rescue, as it were, and made its own money from "Sweet Mother". Prince Nico Mgbarga got his share and was contented under the circumstances.

The absence of reliable patronage affected quite a number of musicians. For instance, Celestine Obiakor who lives near Owerri in Nigeria now lives in abject poverty. Why? Even the broadcasting institution in his country refused to pay him air royalties.

A flashback would inform us that Celestine Obiakor and Herbert

Udemba stepped into the style of the legendary Israel Nwoba. If situations were really ideal for commercial music in Nigeria, would Mr. Obiakor not live on his sweat of yester-years? The only artist who boldly reacted against this sad exploitation was Fela Anikulapo-Kuti, who through his protest, merely scotched the snake and not kill it, while looking for answers to such problems on behalf of performing musicians.

For instance, he was the only artist who demanded for air royalties. He insisted on it until the broadcasting organization blacklisted him and blacked out the use of his works on air and on the television screen. He accepted.

Let us then go through the abridged curriculum vitae of Mike Enahoro, at one time, a performing musician. Mr. Enahoro was described as a "star of the screen" in one of Nigeria's leading magazines, *Top Life*. Since this chapter is devoted to "mini autobiographies" of some performing musicians, indigenous entrepreneurs and music industrialists, we will return to *Top Life* for a cull from an interview with Mike Enahoro.

Mr. Enahoro discussed his early days soon after studying at St. Gregory's College. His father, he said, had different plans for each of his children. He wanted Mike to become a medical doctor or a lawyer but Mr. Enahoro's ambition was to become a "showbiz-man." At school, Mike "gained a reputation, as a school guitar-player" and even acted as instructor to many of his school-mates who shared that interest with him, including Victor Uwaifo. He then presented a most striking background of himself revealing that of a youth who was rebelling against the imposition of classical professional disciplines.

Since Mike's father "vowed not to give him any financial assistance" just for him to become a showbiz-man; Mr. Enahoro ironically determined to uphold the reputation of the Enahoro family, regardless. With his impressive record in sports like soccer and golf, the qualities of adventure, courage, craftsmanship, sportsmanship and strategy would crystallize in his ambition to stay with the arts.

Phase one of his plans, *ab initio,* was to exploit his talents fully as a performing musician. Through this he would guarantee himself self-funding, from his savings, for formal professional education in England. He would also, as a performing musician, establish a foundation for public and self-appraisal, in the art of showbiz.

Mr. Enahoro admitted though that "Idioro, which was the rendezvous of musicians in Lagos, was at that time the downtown Harlem. It housed prostitutes, pimps, drug peddlers and addicts, armed robbers... with pocket knives" Mike's family background, you would say, was his protective device." So, he would, of course, in spite of closeness to these infamous neighbours associate with excellence only. Thus, he "played with renowned musicians such as Bobby Benson, Victor Olaiya, Bill Friday, Zeal Onyia and Roy Chicago."

Mr. Enahoro recalled that his greatest achievement was his contract with Roy Chicago as a guitar player. Two song-texts (and their rhythms) which enhanced Roy Chicago's era in limelight were written by Mike Enahoro. The two songs were "*Eshin O wewu*" and "Maria."

As a musician, Mike was earning J20 a month with approximate extra cash of J20 from fans during their shows within a given month. According to him, consideration for fatter income was also vital to his decision to turn a performing musician taking into account not only that, in civil service, his counterparts earned J20 as their monthly salary, but that he had to earn enough to make a saving for further studies in radio and TV abroad.

In spite of his "break-away" from the Enahoro family at the level of choice of career, his respect for his father and the family encouraged him to focus an the heights. This was not merely to retain a link with his aristocratic roots, but to associate with excellence which his father stood for.

His vision which made reconciliation easy was guided by sportsmanship as evident in this account by *Top Life*:

> Meanwhile, Enahoro was watching his bank account with keen interest... By 1959, the account was heavy enough to enable him go ahead with his plans. He got himself a passport and completed all other necessary arrangements to travel to England by sea.

With deserved elation, Mr. Enahoro discloses: "my brother, Chief Anthony Enahoro, was very pleased with me when he realized how long I had plans to go abroad for studies. He aided me with over £1,000 and remarked that he never thought I was responsible enough to work on such a good idea."

Mike Enahoro then concluded rather triumphantly: "my father, who was initially opposed to my going into showbiz, became very proud of me before his death."

And now, as co-ordinating director (managing director), Mike has arrived at the top of the starting point in his quest for excellence in staffing and programming of Nigerian Television. Mr. Enahoro admits: "the right moment came when I was able to get financial backers and professional hands to make my idea a reality with the establishment of Nationwide Television Enterprises on 1 June 1980." The hopes of indigenous performing musicians partly depend on the innovations expected in the music industry by those who have left their footprints on the performance of popular music, like Mr. Mike Enahoro.

Chernoff provided an elaborate list of some names in African popular music, thus recording Fela Anikulapo-Kuti, Sonny Okosun, Victor Uwaifo as Nigerian "innovative composers." He also listed Osita Osadebe, Celestine Ukwu (who had passed away), Prince Nico Mgbarga, Rex Lawson (of blessed memory), Oliver de Coque and others separately as Nigerian "highlife musicians." Chernoff's list is useful, but we must emphasize that the innovation by Fela Anikulapo-Kuti, Sonny Okosun and Victor Uwaifo is an index of the aesthetic growth of highlife music as we inferred earlier on.

A significant conclusion from Chernoff's study, which is highly applicable to the theme of this work, is his observation that "the tradition of using songs to express philosophical, ethical or satirical themes is unquestionably part of African musical idioms..." Indeed, even contemporary economic problems in Africa, make culture a political tool which promotes and destroys art.

In presenting these autobiographical statements, we have not attempted any order of importance and significance. It is rather an instinctive arrangement, establishing a queue of memories.

## E. C. Arinze

E.C. Arinze is the founding band-master of the legendary Lagos-based Empire Rhythm Orchestra (sets One - Four). The man who made K.K.D (Kakadu) -a Lagos-based nightclub- turn into a magic spot, thus casting a spell on even diplomats, top business executives and public service chief executives:

> I have always been a promoter of national consciousness, Nigerian culture and the arts. That's why in the early sixties, I encouraged Victor Uwaifo (who served me as a young dynamic and potential master guitarist for five good years) to do his first recording in Edo (Binin) language with my musical instruments and lead vocalist. My Recording Company, Decca, had turned down his bid to record, so I gave him Etim Udoh, my alto saxophonist and Exxie Ohunts for a recording at Phillips.

They picked up other talents and that was the birth of the first Nigerian 'Pick-Ups,' just to record Victor Uwaifo's songs.

After the Nigerian Civil War, the rehabilitation of my musical instruments for the Drum Room of Hotel Presidential, Enugu, was generously paid for by a one-time Nigerian permanent Representative at the United Nations, Chief Dr. Edwin Ogbu.

I could claim to be the first artist in Nigeria in the fifties recorded by Decca in a rented room at Ebute Metta in Lagos. The room was converted into an improvised recording studio. Ordinary thick papers were plastered on the walls of the room to serve as sound-proof. Decca used mobile recording equipment. The rest were done in London. Their first recording engineer in Nigeria was Mr. Bannister.

I won a Decca award of an expensive engraved trumpet which cost about £350 (three hundred and fifty British pounds) then. I still use it till today.

I'm happy I have been able to create a night-club consciousness for Enugu with my experiments at the Drum Room of Hotel Presidential there.

I'm indebted to Steve Rhodes for teaching me how to read music during the N.B.S. Dance Time on air in those days. I'm indebted to Chief Bank-Anthony, Chief Dr. Edwin Ogbu and others who were my top fans and 'patrons' at the Magic Spot (K.K.D). I shall always remember Justice Nkemena for encouraging me to go professional when the proprietor of Empire Rhythm Orchestra, Abel Kanu, approached me in 1953.

As a leader of the first set of Empire Rhythm Orchestra, We were probably the first dance-band used in the earliest programmes of the first television station in Nigeria, WNTV, Ibadan, during the days of Steve Rhodes and Emmanuel Omitshade as executives of WNBS-WNTV.

For the popular West African Carnival, known as

Havana Nite, run by Sigma Club at University College, Ibadan (U.C.I); I could claim that my presentation of 'Oh my Papa' brought recognition to Nigerian dance-bands and began to de-emphasize the Club's policy of importing bands from Ghana. On that special evening, I alternated with E.T. Mensah of Ghana at Tromakerd Hall/Tower Court stage."

Bobby Benson and Willie Payne were the greatest influence I had when I moved from brass-band instruments to "orchestral" instruments. I spent quite some time watching them play at the nightclubs where they demonstrated their skills before I took off with the Empire Rhythm Orchestra. The number of talented musicians grew and I saw the need for splitting into sets. Steve Rhodes was a judge of the first knock-out competition which made me leader of the first set and Eric Onugha, leader of the second set. I invited Steve Amechi to be leader of the third set and brought in a former teacher of mine, of St. Peter's School Band in Enugu, to lead set four. He is Agu Norris.

My full names are Eliezer Chukwuwetalu Arinze. I am from Uga-Amuna in Obosi, Anambra State of Nigeria. I could claim that my first inspiration to turn a musician was during my childhood. My mother was a Christian. She was a singer in the choir, the guilds and so on. My uncle was an organist. I always held the lantern for him in the early hours of the day whenever he rehearsed his organ. I learnt to play the flute and the mouth organ under him. Even when he was transferred to Ogwashi-Uku and Onitsha-Olona in his ministerial work under C.M.S., I still accompanied him even to Agbor-Obi -all in Delta State of Nigeria. But by far, the greatest background I had was my role in St. Peters Band, Ogbete in Enugu when I was schooling at St. Peters. That was where I met Agu Norris who was a teacher then. I was very much involved with the band, when I was in elementary five as a pupil.

    I was also involved in Central School Band at Obosi when I was sent back home by an uncle of mine, an official of the Coal Mine, who couldn't stand the idea of my turning a musician.

After my primary education, I was admitted to the Teachers Training College at Obosi but Mr. Oruchalu, an educationist, was very interested in my interest in music. So, upon completing my T. T. C. course, Mr. Iloabachie, a well-known educationist, got me moved to Central School (C.M.S.), Onitsha where I led the school band. Right from Obosi, I had begun to accept little contracts to play at marriages, etc. What gave me pride was that I led the school band to the last Empire Day celebrations in 1950 at Onitsha. All these were in mid-forties.

But a significant date was 3 September, 1953, when at Agbor in Delta State, as I still tagged on to my organist-uncle, I was invited by one Mr. Abel Kanu, a well-known Lagos-based hotelier, to come to Lagos and make the musical instruments he imported operational with a live band. I hesitated, but Mr. Justice Nkemena, an "uncle" so to speak (he is from Obosi) encouraged me. A contract was signed and I went to Lagos on the monthly salary of 140 (forty pounds).

It is important to note that while at Onitsha, what we used was the brass band which had actually produced talents in music -Stephen Amechi was one of them. He was a product of Africa College at Onitsha. Both Bethel and Africa Colleges at Onitsha had done a lot to produce musicians with their college bands. Victor Olaiya and Eddie Okonta were also products of Africa College. Chris Odiase was a young instrument teacher there.

Before I arrived at Lagos, Empire Hotel, like many other hotels in Lagos, hired the services of visiting European bands; "Hot Shots" was then Empire Hotel's visiting band. I went to Lagos with a handful of ex-students of Bethel and Africa Colleges.

The popular music then in Nigeria was "marriage." Mr. Magnus Iwowari, an accountant, was really the brain behind the logistics for a resident band for Empire Hotel. When we took off, one Okeiyi was the drummer. I decided on some strategy - to watch the most popular nightclub musicians then as my models; such models would form two resident bands for Empire Hotel. It was necessary for the bands to be at least two. This is because there was a regular demand by the public, for hiring the resident band of Empire Hotel, obviously because of its reputation. It was Magnus Iwowari who named the band 'Empire Rhythm Orchestra.' The two most popular musicians were Bobby Benson, playing at Alfred Rewani's nightclub named Rex Club and Willie Payne of "Mambo Dance" fame at Universal Club at Yaba. Steve Rhodes was a judge of our knock-out competition which gave me the pride of place as leader of Empire Rhythm Orchestral's First Set and Eric Onugha, a very talented musician, as leader of Second Set.

Later on, as the demands for engagements (by which I mean contracts for servicing clients) grew, there was need for a Third Set. I sent for Mr. Stephen Amechi, a great talent. He arrived in Lagos and led our Third Set. Abel Kanu, decided to bring back "Chief Billy Friday" from Ghana to lead a Fourth Set. Unfortunately for Chief Billy Friday (of blessed memory), Agu Norris, a teacher in my former elementary school at St. Peter's Ogbete in Enugu, who was involved with the school band, as I was, as Elementary Five Pupil, had indicated an interest in joining Empire Rhythm Orchestra. As a first step, I got him to head the resident band of Central Hotel Dugbe, at Ibadan. The hotel was owned by one top politician, Kern. After a spell with the Central Hotel band at Ibadan, Agu Norris still indicated interest to serve Empire Rhythm Orchestra. I was dodging because I felt embarrassed to have him serve under me whereas I was a pupil when he was already a teacher in my elementary school, as mentioned earlier on. Anyway, while competing with Chief Bill Friday, I won the toss for Agu Norris to become leader of the Fourth Set of Empire Rhythm Orchestra.

Among the contracts for engagements which followed our rising popularity at Empire Rhythm Orchestra were those from (1) Ikeja Arms Hotel run by a European, Mr. John Harold (who was the proprietor and his European manager, Mr. Smith); (2)

Ikeja Country Club (also a European exclusive). And I will even include my engagement when I turned independent in 1959; (3) W.N.B.S-WNTV, Ibadan; (4) Sigma Club's Havana Nite where I played along side E. T. Mensah and his Tempos Band of Ghana. It was my presentation of "Oh, my Papa" at Havana Nite that began to de-emphasize the need for Sigma Club, to go out for Ghanaian bands. Of course, other Nigerian bands emerged after.

I can claim to be the first or one of the few pioneering artists for Decca in Nigeria because I was "rated" as Number One Dance-Band then. I played mixed rhythms suitable for ballroom dance. I wish to re-emphasize that Decca established an improvised small-room-recording studio at Ebute Metta with Mr. Bannister, an Englishman, as the first recording engineer. They recorded on portable equipment. The finish of the work was carried out in London for the fragile gramophone discs then, plastic singles and extended plays which followed. My first number with Decca was entitled "*Fa analum okwum-o.*"

## Chris Ajilo

Outside world now looks towards Africa for new materials. We would like to encourage Nigerian artists that we could sell overseas instead of recording Nigerian artists imitating those who expect to have materials from us.

Our music will be sold outside this country if we can actually present African music or Nigerian music in its true colour without bastardizing it.

And one of this music we should be proud of is highlife ... it is typically a West African music ... the rhythm is as important as the lyrical lines; it has to be meaningful; it just has to have a message...

It is the musician as a creator who produces music as an art for recording companies and as a piece of work for critical analysis by the musicologist...

I owe Nigeria the responsibility of training instrumentalists and musicians. My satisfaction comes from that...that is why I lingered for long on my own before joining Polygram as producer staff.

I was born in Lagos. My parents are from Oyo State in Nigeria. I have been spending all my life in Lagos except for my many years of music study and practical experience in London and other parts of Britain; as well as eight years in Ibadan upon my return to Nigeria in 1955. I am not a Brazillian as some think.

Between 1943 and 1953, I was educated at C.M.S Grammar School, Lagos; Birmingham Technical College, England; Central School of Music, London; and Eric Gilder School of Music, London. Thus, I hold a Diploma from Central School of Music in London, majoring in Saxophone and Clarinet; a Certificate from Eric Gilder in general musicianship; and a Certificate from Royal School of Music in theory of music.

I am particularly proud to say that I understood music theory and arrangement under the celebrated music teacher, Eric Gilder himself. Distinguished teachers of music like Johnny Dankworth, Kenny Graham and Aubrey Franks tutored me in saxophone, clarinet and flute.

I have held several appointments. I was music teacher at St. John's School, Lagos; Director of Music, "Nigerian Institute of Music" Lagos; Director of Art, Alade Music Show programme of Nigerian Television (now Nigerian Television Authority) Lagos; Leader of the Preachers Band; instructor in instrumental music at International Secondary School of Ibadan University; Resident Band Leader at Lafia Hotel and Premier Hotel -both at Ibadan in Nigeria.

I was flutist and clarinetist with the Ibadan Operatic Society in many operatic productions. I was composer, saxophonist and clarinetist at El Morroco Night Club, Excelsior Hotel, Apapa; I also went on tour of the USSR; I was the resident bandleader of the Cubanos at Federal Palace Hotel, Victoria Island, Lagos; and also resident band leader at the Mainland Hotel in Lagos.

I was leader, Assistant Conductors, Tenor Saxophonist and clarinetist with the N.B.C. Dance Orchestra in Lagos under the conductorship of the celebrated musicologist, Fela Sowande. I toured West Africa with my band -Chris Ajilo & His Cubanos; with the same band I performed at the Latin Quarters, West End, London. In 1953, I did a summer work with Arthur Rowbury's Band at Astoria, Nottingham, England.

Festivals have also exploited my artistry. During Second World Black & African Festival of Arts and culture (styled FESTAC '77), I was artist-trainer for the Nigerian National Band and Popular Music. Back in 1960, I was leader of Nigerian National Orchestra for the State Ball during Nigerian Independence Celebration.

Among my compositions are "Only You," Angola," "The Falling Hero," "Ariwo," "Emi Mimo," "Tete De," "Nigeria Calling," "Afufu," "Lafia Jump," "Eko O gba gbere," "Ojo Nlo" and "Emi Mimo."

The importance of research is not missing in my work. I own many tapes resulting from my research on traditional/modern instrumentation combination of goje, piano, calabash and flute. My researches were recorded on tape by the Nigerian Broadcasting Corporation under the expert supervision of Fela Sowande. I actually play most Nigerian musical instruments and I take time off to walk, swim and dance.

Upon my return to Nigeria in the mid-fifties, I was so popular that my hair style became popular and fashionable. Barbers did Ajilo hair-do. Bicycle repairers tagged Ajilo style at the workshops. My fans cut across class-hierarchy.

After many years in Britain, I was, of course, overpowered by nostalgia. I had trained the late Alhaji Anifowose at Birmingham. I therefore arranged that he return to Nigeria before me; and upon return, organize a band. He did, and the band was operational at Island Club and Yoruba Tennis club in Lagos. Thus, when I returned on 15 January 1955, there was a "ready-made" band to lead the same night at West-End Cafe in Lagos.

Way back in England, the band was already named "Cool Cats Band" at Birmingham, playing every Sunday. Kazul Anifowose was the author of that name. My relationship with music at birth could be tied-up with the coincidence of my birthday. I was born on Boxing Day. Thus, I was born into merriment and music.

## Bala Miller

Bala Miller is the founder and the first principal of the defunct School of Music, Kano, Nigeria.

In academics, all our people think about is Ph.D; and when they get it most of them have nothing to show for it practically in their area of discipline.

I am interested in the development of music and musicians in Africa.

African music has no counterpoint to the listener whose ears are not trained to appreciate its aesthetic and philosophical qualities.

I was an executive with Ports Authority, Breweries, Commercial Firms, etc until I founded the Kano School of Music.
I am from Zaria, which some in Nigeria simply refer to as University town."
My father was one of the early Hausa Christians. He did his divinity course at Oshogbo and St. Andrew's College, Oyo, both in the former Western Nigeria. He was ordained a priest along with the late Dr. Lucas, Rev. Ocheku, and Rev. Bako, who is the only one among them still living. My own father died on 19 December, 1966.
Being a missionary, you were automatically tied up with music because in those days, the missionary was also the church organist, the choirmaster, the teacher and the catechist -he was everything. Thus, by sheer co-incidence, I was born into music.

I started studying music at an early age. I also started singing with the church choir.

Eventually, my father was transferred to Lokoja in 1932. The C.M.S School at Lokoja -Holy Trinity School- was the first elementary school built in the North of Nigeria by the late Bishop Ajayi Crowther around 1875.

The former Government of Nigeria was then situated at Lokoja before the British Niger Company took over that area when the Government seat moved. The British colonial army at Lokoja sold or handed over a set of musical instruments to the Church Missionary Society School. Thus when my father transferred to Lokoja with us, the School there already possessed a band comprising bass drums, side drums, comet trombone, etc.

I was first attracted to highlife music when 1 listened to "*Yabunsa*" recorded by Tunde King between "1937 and 1939." "*Yabunsa*" was then very popular. In later years that song was popularized by Ghana's E.T. Mensah, Nigeria's Victor Olaiya and even Rex Lawson who produced it in Kalabari language, his mother tongue in Nigeria.

I was lucky to be a member of the school band. I learnt how to play musical instruments by watching others play. I had the advantage of living with the musical instruments since by the position of my father; the band-set was under his custody for security. By 1937, at the age of nine, I was already able to play the trumpet and the shorter trumpet called the comet as well as the flute, which was the instrument officially assigned to me. But my mastery of trumpet surprised many fans. Thus, during the coronation of Britain's Queen Elizabeth the second's father in 1937, I was proud to be named a member of the School band to join in the coronation celebrations in Nigeria.

I was eleven years old when the World War broke out in 1939, 1 was already proficient in the trumpet and the cornet. Thus, in that same year when a prominent member of the Church, one Mr. Roberts, a Lagosian, donated a trumpet to the school, I was the only one bold enough to demonstrate a show with it. Most of the other boys could play the comet. They dreaded the trumpet as human beings tend to dread a change of the "old order."

In 1943, as providence would have it, my father was transferred to Lagos to take over from Rev. Canon Hunter who was chaplain of the Cathedral Church of Christ. Canon Hunter was transferred to Burma, one of the scenes of the global war, as army Chaplain.

I was now of college age. The Bishop of Lagos, the late Bishop Viney, asked me to make a choice between three schools: King's College, C.M.S Grammar School and Igbobi College. I opted for C.M.S Grammar School for a number of personal reasons. The Bishop persuaded me first for Igbobi College. "No I needed a different school from my older brother's. He was in Igbobi College around 1934." "What of King's College?" "I'm afraid the boys there may not be attending the Church." "They do," my Lord, the Bishop said.

Anyway, my choice was C.M.S Grammar School, the second secondary school in British West Africa; the first was in Sierra Leone. Our badge was Oxford and Cambridge blues. It was situated near my home in Lagos. Kakawa was parallel to Odulami street where C.M.S School was. We used to snub King's College boys until I became friendly with Sam Akpabot (now Professor Akpabot), who became a chorister at the Cathedral Church of Christ and I also got acquainted, on the soccer field, with Alex Ekwueme (later Dr. Alex Ekwueme and former Vice President of Federal Republic of Nigeria).

Music was a compulsory subject at C.M.S Grammar School from preps one to class three. That school has produced eminent musicians and musicologists: Akin Euba, most of the Bucknors, Yinka Holly, Oluwale, Art Alade, all of whom, at the age of ten, were already good pianists. Also, Christopher Oyesiku who later joined the Nigerian Broadcasting Corporation (or Service?). Most homes I was connected with then in Lagos owned pianos.

I did not consider myself a successful music student. I was over curious and inquisitive. I never accepted any music doctrine without demanding the logic which led to any formula. What is the difference between E flat and D sharp for instance? The two are the same, or are they not. A good number of my music subject teachers were angry with me but Bishop Carley, the school principal was very understanding. I stayed at school even during the holidays, practising with the piano and the organ. I was allowed that liberty.

In 1948, we decided to raise some fund for our school. A concert show would be ideal or, in fact, a drama-music variety. By now, Bishop Carley was away to Britain. The show was produced under Rev. Adelaja. At that time the vogue was jazz; so, we decided on Glenn Miller's "*Chatanooga Choo Chod*" and went across to the Salvation Army School opposite us to borrow a trumpet. To add greater action, G.O.K. Ajayi, now a celebrated Nigerian lawyer, Ganiyu Davies and I thrilled the audience with a jitterbug, as a kind of "side show." T.O.S. Benson, later a well-known politician, was the chairman of the occasion since he himself was an old boy of C.M.S Grammar School. He was so impressed by our show that he offered to give me a lift to and from the school for a full one year since we were also next door neighbours. I also suspected he had an eye on me as a potential musician for his brother's jam-session orchestra. (His brother was Bobby Benson).

I later joined the "Calabar Brass Band" in Lagos. We played in the streets like it was done in the streets of New Orleans in the United States of America. We played for marriages and functions and occasions of that nature. It is interesting to recall that we were three trumpeters with two trumpets only to share. Bill Friday, Inyang Ubot and I were the three trumpeters. Our wages were one shilling and six pence monthly and of course, you had to tip the band master with a six pence cigarette or you may not be sure of retaining your job in the band for another show. I needed that extra cash supplement because my father was by now transferred back to the North. At the same time, I was cautious to see that our school authorities did not catch me playing in a dance band.

Upon leaving school, I joined Sam Akpabot's "All-Stars" Band. Soon I became his deputy. My instrument was, of course, the trumpet while Sam's was the saxophone. We had big names like Holloway and Willoughby. Victor Olaiya came from time to time, to add to the strength and quality of our band. Sifo Lawson also came to lend support to the trumpet artistry. Sam Akpabot left for United Kingdom in 1953.

In 1954, a friend, Larinde Cole, requested that I raise a band for his nightclub at the West-End Hotel. I did, and we kept the nightclub going. We played free just for "the kicks" as it were. At this time I was an executive with a commercial firm, the Lever Brothers. I was in their Marketing Department. Thus, there was an inevitable clash between my regular job and the nightclub music hobby. So, I gave-up the nightclub since my flirtation between the two brought a decline to the quality of the nightclub rhythms. I invited Victor Olaiya who at that time led one of the five band sets of Bobby Benson. Olaiya himself was actually an accountant fully employed after his secondary education.

The band boys I was leaving for Victor Olaiya were not too sure about the quality they would expect from anybody from Bobby Benson's outfit whose musicians were regarded as "unpolished." Before Olaiya took over the band, we had decided on "blacklisting" Ghana highlife songs so that we may remain original. Of course, one did not expect E.T. Mensah to be happy with this. Our first popular highlife number was "*Oni dodo, oni moi-moi.*" Cornie Ajilo (Chris Ajilo's sister) joined as vocalist. She told me about Chris Ajilo's musical activities in London where he led an all-White band. Chris was my colleague at C.M.S Grammar School, so I wrote him inviting him to return as we all prepared for the political independence of Nigeria. Certainly, there were challenges and openings for pioneering works; he did return. Another girl, fresh from school with a good school certificate joined Cornie Ajilo as vocalist - that was Catherine Garland. When Chris Ajilo returned, he brought along a Ghanaian, Sammy Lartey (later Director of Music in Ghana Broadcasting Organization) and a drummer, Odeyi, a young man whose home is Oyo.

But it was a young Lagosian Anifowose, who rechristened the West End Night Club band with the name "Cool Cat." The incentives for good nightclub music grew, so I composed the song "*Kusimilaya*" in 1955. "Cool Cat" began attracting responsible and educated young patrons -young lawyers like Rotimi Williams, Fani Kayode, George Nickles (later the Chief executive of Top Beer), Yemi Lawson, Chris Ogubanjo, Sonny Adewale, Mrs. Aduke Moore (nee Alakija). "*Kusimilaya*" became a craze; it was a satire to flush out those who never say what they mean or mean what they say. But the band was making no money; sometimes, the gate fee was seventeen shillings and six pence. At that time, business was not as you would have it. Bobby Benson was better-off because of his rich brother. He persuaded Chris Ajilo to join the jazz group called 'Bens-Ajilo.' They had people like Mike Falana (a clever young trumpeter) who used to play with the band. In 1948, when we went to play at Abeokuta Grammar School, I met Fela and his brother, Beko. Fela was about 10 years old then and he wanted to play the trumpet but I played the trumpet and he played the piano. The policy of our band was "no smoking or drinking on stage, good performance, sense of responsibility, time and punctuality."

Eventually, things went wrong with the band and it was sold. At this time, I was in Jos and the hotel organizations in Jos wanted to merge all the bands and be responsible for paying the musicians. I disagreed because once there is no competition, their standards would fall and they would have no bargaining power. The band in Ambassador Hotel, led by Jim Christian, opted for the merger. Universal Hotel band in Jos, led by Eddyson, did not accept a merger, so I told them to go to Lagos where I recommended them to some men who could help them. Bobby Benson and Victor Olaiya were the obvious backing angels 1 recommended them to, I advised Eddyson and his colleagues to be armed with a repertoir of their own songs. The musicians in Lagos did not co-operate. It was only Zeal Onyia who lent them some instruments which they used in touring from place to place. They got a hundred pounds. They played until they got to Benin and bought their own instruments -Zeal Onyia having demanded his own instruments and recovered them. The group then sent one of its members to Jos to tell me that they had formed a band. They brought some suggestions about names for the band and I told them the names sounded too English and since they started from the North, they should take a name that goes with the North. The two names I suggested to them were "Pyramids of the North" (to reflect the groundnut pyramids) or "The Sahara." They accepted "The Sahara" which later became "Sahara All-Stars" upon their return to Benin. Victor Olaiya was not too happy that "all stars" were attached to that name since his own band was named with all-stars, but 1 argued that no one had an exclusive right to that name. Victor, of course, added the phrase "international" to give a distinction to the name of his band.

In 1966, I went to Lagos to pick up a job. The Ports Authority Chief knew enough about me and my music. He requested me to raise a band for Ports Authority. I produced one just within three days. As the band played, the General Manager could not believe it. He was overwhelmed by the speed with which I produced the band and named "The Harbours."

## Inyang Henshaw

The "velvet-voice." The royal Efik musician; Talent-Scout; Studio Manager Artists & Repertoir Manager to Phillips West Africa Records Company, Lagos, Nigeria; and later, Instructor of cultural music at the University of Calabar.

Ekpo Ekpenyong -a seaman and a friend of mine was the one who recommended me to Bobby Benson at Liverpool in England just before Bobby returned to

Nigeria in 1947.

I arrived Enugu in 1949 and revived the Eastern New Time orchestra in 1950 upon the request of the owner of the dance-band, a timber contractor.

Bobby Benson let me go on my own merit.

With a tour which took the band to Kano, I founded the 'Rendezvous Dandies Orchestra' for Abdul Wada upon his negotiation with Francis Bourdoux, my Enugu-based employer.

All types of music in Nigeria will come and go but the only one that will never die is highlife. Highlife music has come to stay.

E.T. Mensah of Ghana played highlife with a striking difference...A lot of people in Nigeria tried to copy his style ...1 myself did...Bobby was more concerned with the kind of music which interpreted his theatrical shows...

I started as a chorister of the Duke Town Church Choir in my home, Calabar in Nigeria. I was later transferred to Henshaw Town Church Choir where I distinguished myself in singing competitions with the choir of other churches. It was actually Mr. Ekanem who took singing classes that discovered my talent at Duke Town School.
   But it was Mr. Ekeng Ita, the choirmaster of Henshaw Town Church Choir who negotiated my transfer from Duke Town Church Choir to Henshaw Town Church Choir. In both places, I was the lead voice.
   One Ekpo Ekpenyong -a seamen and a friend of mine met Bobby Benson at Liverpool just when Bobby was about to return to Nigeria. He found out that Bobby would set up a theatrical business or showbiz when he settled down back in Nigeria. So, he recommended me to him.
   Bobby Benson called on me in Lagos where I was now staying with my uncle. My mother received

him in my absence. I was to meet him and have a business chat, which I did. I was working in the Nigerian Railways then.

Bobby employed me and got me to teach songs I had written. His major partner was his wife, Cassandra. What Bobby started was a kind of theatrical group called 'Bobby-Cassandra Group' in 1947. We even toured the whole country, including Calabar. His elder brother, T.O.S. Benson was then a Customs Officer. He in fact advised Bobby to get an orchestra attached to his theatre group, like Hubert Ogunde's. T.O.S Benson then purchased the band-set popularly known as the 'Jam-Session Orchestra' in 1948. We were based at the Yaba Race Club in Lagos. I was second in command to Bobby.

A request came from Enugu, brought by one Francis Bourdoux, a friend of Bobby's, who needed a talented musician to revive his "Eastern New Time Orchestra." It was an open competition for all of us in Bobby's group. I won the "toss" to go to Enugu and I did in 1950.

Eastern New Time Orchestra undertook a tour which took us to Kano. At Kano, one Abdul Wada was so much in love with my dance music that he requested that I and the band stay back in Kano as a resident band. I contacted Francis Bourdoux at Enugu and he came to Kano and negotiated with Abdul Wada. So, we stayed back in Kano for ten good years, 1950 - 1960.

In 1961, I founded my own dance-band and named it "Top Ten Aces." I had really developed as a composer. Highlife music was my main concentration but, in those days a ball-room dance involved Waltz, Blues, Foxtrot, Tango, etc., which we handled beautifully.

I am a member of the International Performing Rights Society. That means that you send the songs you have written abroad to be registered. Culture feeds my music mainly and that brings along with it other ideas.

I took an appointment with Phillips West Africa Records Company in Lagos as a Studio Manager. That job did not affect the quality of my "Top Ten Aces" band which I still kept in action. My first recording was actually on 'Patsol' (Patrick Solomon) label and it was popular.

Now, I am an instructor at the Department of Theatre Arts, University of Calabar. So, I am really back home. I teach the students cultural music. I am no longer as flamboyant as I was in my younger years, which, is natural.

For the University, I work according to schedule. I impart as much knowledge as I can and as they can take from my own experience. The students appreciate that someone like me is there to show them what they don't know and to brush up what they already know. I may even call my own area for the students "a new intellectual horizon." The students are enthusiastic.

The late Kingsley Bassey was the one closest to my style. He was leading the "Moonlight Professionals." He copied my style almost to the core. He stayed with my type of music in highlife. All types of popular music in Nigeria will come and go. But the only one that will never die is highlife. Highlife music has come to stay. I am not interested in the controversy about the origin of highlife between Nigeria and Ghana. All I know is that there was highlife music in Nigeria before E.T. Mensah of Ghana toured Nigeria when I was still at school. But I must admit that he played highlife with a striking difference as I listened to him. A lot of people in Nigeria tried to copy E.T. Mensah's style. When I became a composer and led a band, I copied E.T Mensah's style.

I cannot really credit Bobby Benson with introducing a new style of highlife in Nigeria because he was more concerned with the kind of music which interpreted his theatrical shows.

I met E.T. Mensah before my association with Bobby's Jam-Session Orchestra. Baby-Face Paul also joined us; Zeal Onyia was picked up at Warri when he was still at school. He also lived with Malory, the owner of the Race Club at Yaba.

Zeal Onyia later went to study in London. When he returned, he joined the Nigerian Broadcasting Corporation in Lagos. Baby-Face Paul died in London.

He had released some "albums" and was becoming very popular.

Victor Olaiya, Zeal Onyia and quite a few of our colleagues were really popular with the people. They played what people liked to listen to and dance to as well.

As I said earlier on although a number of Nigerian musicians copied E. T. Mensah's style, they still stamped their own ethnic and cultural images on the style.

Highlife music actually drew from traditional highlife rhythms like Juju in the defunct Western Nigeria, Itembe from the Efik peoples, Shatta and Gwoje from the North. So, highlife music is an extraction from traditional rhythms and cultural music of the people. E. T. Mensah's Nigerian tour influenced the growth of a number of highlife musicians in Nigeria.

Efik cultural music influenced me richly. I used to go to our plantations, when I was at school, to spend my holidays with my aunt who was a palm-oil production contractor. In the evening, after the plantation settlers had returned from hunting and fanning, they sat round to relax with folklore and fables. I keenly listened to them and participated enthusiastically.

But those folklore and fables did not mean much more to me than entertainment until I left school. I began recalling them and making notes which led to my compositions, which I taught my band.

My lyrics are drawn from Efik cultural folklore. Of course, the Efiks are very beautiful singers; they possess what I may call "natural close harmony" when they form themselves into singing groups.

When I joined the "White Star Musical Party" which started in the forties and was led by one Mr. Archibong, I contributed immensely but learnt more from the group because they sang very nice tunes. Their repertory was packed with cultural themes, but had a lot to do with the sufferings of the people, life, death and love.

I would always give credit for my real understanding of music to the church. It was in the church choir I learnt my "tonic solfe" etc. My church was Church of Scotland Mission (now Presbyterian). I picked up ideas from roadside ceremonies, e.t.c so they too were also my sources.

I.K. Dairo, Ebenezer Obey, Sunny Ade and others play what one would call "indigenous or church brotherhood dance band highlife." If you added more instruments to their set, their music converts to modern highlife music.

The recording industry has done a lot to project Nigerian popular music. The industry has enhanced the development of music. Indigenisation of the music industry also was a healthy thing. Recording acted as a preserver of musical talents and left them as an artistic legacy even when the live-performance has long been forgotten.

Israel Nwoba, Mamman Shatta, Dan Maraya and others like them also played what is akin to highlife one way or the other. You may call their style traditional highlife. That style is still noticeable when one listens even today to Dan Maraya and Mamman Shatta of the North, who are still alive.

1 am unable to give more details about Patsol Recording Industry at Calabar, but my own record with that label, as I said earlier on sold out. Patsol had no branches outside Calabar, so when it packed up, that was the end.

The Nigerian musical scene was really active as I recall names like Rex Lawson, Joe Nez, Eddie Okonta, Okonkwo Adigwe, Baby-Face Paul etc. All of them had their own personal identity or image in their style of highlife music.

Music has no language or if you like, music has international language, thus it has international appeal. So, part of my crusade was to spread highlife beyond the borders of Nigeria. If that was a dream, I realized it.

The only time I felt that my dreams of spreading highlife was shattering was during the terrible days of active partisan politics in 1950. That was in Kano during the political campaigns which led to our independence. Action Group and NCNC clashed. There was a free fight among the political party members and fans. This was at the hotel where we were playing. I had no alternative but to flee and find my way out through the fence which blocked the hotel from trespassers. I remained very popular with my shows.

## Chief Stephen Osita Osadebe
*A manufacturer of highlife stars*

I won't say we musicians in Nigeria have done enough... our modern musicians are more on pop and disco-rock music. They lay more emphasis on love music than on the ones that will help remedy the situation in the country.

There are a thousand and one ways of reducing the problems facing our country. Music could be effectively used. The only thing that remains is this: the person you talked to, did it enter his ears and what did he do with it after hearing?
Musicians are trying very much. They are saying what should be done and will continue saying it, until they are done.

My father is Dennis Obi Osadebe, from Atani (Umueke Village). I was born in Onitsha on March 17, 1936. I spent my childhood in Onitsha. I was named Louis Ositedinma. I schooled at St. John's Catholic School, Onitsha. I did classes one, two and standard one all in the same year. After primary school, my late uncle, Christopher Osadebe, put me in College (Africa College). I did two years there. My uncle could no longer afford to pay my school fees due to financial problems. I had to stop schooling. I was put under my uncle's working place in ACU. I worked there as a clerk.
As for music, in the first place; in Atani Village, music is in our land. My father was a popular musician and dancer so was my mother and one of my uncles called Dibia Anyaoji, who died in December, 1983. My nickname was Dibia Azaka and I am a strongly-built man. Also, when I was at school I

was among the choral group and the school band. Although I did not attend any musical school, I saw that I was very talented in music. In our Odo-akpu community (Onitsha), there was a traditional dance called *Amakekwu, Kokoma*, etc and I was among the participants. I was very popular in it to the extent that if there was a traditional marriage ceremony, and the group happens to play for the occasion, if I was not present the dance group is regarded as incomplete. I was then known and called Louis but now I am being addressed as Stephen. It is because my school at that time was owned by the Catholic Mission and had a decree that unless one has received the sacrament of Baptism, one should not answer an English name. At the time I was baptized in 1949, 1 had an uncle named Stephen and because I liked that name, I chose it as my baptismal name, also, in 1950 when we were about to be confirmed, I chose another uncle's name (my father's elder brother) Patrick, as my confirmation name.

While under employment, I got to like Ghanaian music, Congo music, etc. At one time, a band headed by one Mr. Stephen Amechi, came from Lagos. I went to their show and saw the vocalist singing a traditional tune. I thought that the vocalist was not singing it properly and that I could do it better. So I went to one of my own kinsmen called David Ijoma from Atani (he is now dead) who was with the band, and told him that I could sing better than that vocalist. David went and told Stephen who then asked me to come and sing one of their compositions. I went and sang the song, after which David asked me to come to Lagos, promising that he will help me become one of the members of the band.

During that time, I was good at playing the Conga. So I went to Lagos with some money given to me by my uncle, Christopher. 1 stayed in Lagos for four months without getting the job of a vocalist with the band. So I came back and continued my work at ACU. I was first employed there in 1956 and worked until December, 1957 and resigned, with the resolution that I wanted to be a musician. But my father disagreed while my uncle, Chris, supported me because it's what I wanted to do. In March 1958, my uncle gave me money and I went to Lagos again. I arrived at Lagos an Easter Monday 1958 and Stephen Amechi welcomed me into his group. I was given the maraca to play and I did it quite well. Their vocalist wasn't quite good. Stephen commissioned me to do the vocals as well as the maraca during their nightly shows. I stayed 3 months with the band.

Central Hotel was then opened in Lagos. It was owned by a certain businessman from Nkwerre in the former Eastern Nigeria. His name was Chief Osuani. His band leader was known as Eric Onugha. Eric came and took me from Stephen Amechi and put me in their band at Central Hotel. My salary was #4 (four pounds) monthly when I was with Stephen Amechi's band, but Eric's band paid me double and that was #8 (eight pounds) monthly. I regarded that as a promotion because I was taken from the post of a maraca-player to that of a frontline vocalist, even with more pay. I started then to copy and sing songs from Ghana. At that time, the custom was that bands played mixed music. I also copied and sang European songs, as well as my own traditional music.

Then there were political problems in N.C.N.C known in full as National Council of Nigeria and the Camerouns. At that time, Zik, Balogun and Mbadiwe's misunderstandings pushed me to produce a traditional tune, telling them to come together and unite so that Nigeria would have good leadership. That was my first original composition. The flip side of that record was "*Adamma I gbue m egbue*" (Adamma, you have killed me). The record was produced under the Central Hotel Band (i.e. Eric's band). Many people loved it and bought it. Hubert Ogunde and Zeal Onyia came. Zeal was then doing some recording for Hubert Ogunde. Zeal loved me and so he took me from my residence where I was paying £4 (four pounds) a month and put me in his own flat. He helped me with my songs; he used his trumpet to teach me how to sing my vocals. Eventually, I composed some songs which Zeal rehearsed with his own band and was recorded at Ogunde's studio. The first of the songs was "*No*

*Money, no woman,*" the second was a Calabar song, the third was "*Ezinne*" (good mother). The record was produced in Zeal's name because I had no band then. The album sold a great deal.

Hubert Ogunde then made a contract with me which gave me the responsibility of making record albums for Ogunde. So I began by picking instrumentalists from different bands owned by hoteliers. We do the rehearsals in the hotel and record at Ogunde's studio. The first album I did on Ogunde's label was "*Lagos Life, na so so enjoyment*" recorded at Ogunde's studio. It sold very much and many people came to me for contract to write songs for music albums on their own labels or as producers. I did many of them.

I was the Assistant General Secretary of the Musicians Union. The General Secretary of the Musicians Union was a trained man in Labour Law. Since the government lost him to the union, they decided to replace him. So, I was chosen by the government to go overseas to do "a course in Labour Law." I was sent to Moscow in Russia, I came back in 1962.

I still did not quit music. After work, I would go to the Radio Station, at the time when Professor S. Akabogu was there, for some programmes. They usually called on me to do some songs for them during one of their programmes.

Later on, things went wrong in another political party, the Nigerian Peoples Congress. The situation went out of control, so I quit the civil service. I then concentrated on radio programmes. By that time, I hadn't formed a band of my own, but I had made a name in the music world in Nigeria even by the first record bearing my own group's name called the "Nigeria Sound Makers Band." But it was by collecting people from other bands that I made that album. I pay them immediately after recording and took my own share. After some time, I got enough money and bought musical instruments which I used to play my music. Then I formed my own band in 1964. My first contract as a band owner was in Onitsha with the owner of Central Hotel, Onitsha, known as Chief L.

Anadu from Agu-Ukwu, who had business in Lagos and was based there. From then onwards, I had my own musicians and got my commission from Chief Anadu, who pays me also for producing albums for him. That was how I kept on from 1964 in Onitsha till this day.

When one listens to my music, all I say appear meaningful, at times they are in the form of proverbs which provoke much thought afterwards. When I was young, I used to stay with elderly people (my uncles). I listen to whatever they say. I was gifted with a feeling of knowing or feeling what is going to happen in the future through the behaviour of people, so I try to talk to the people against their bad character and their consequence. I say what should be done, the time to do it and at what it should not be done. Whenever I do so, some people tend to take it that there is enmity between me and somebody and that I am preaching against that person. But what I preach against usually happens and it becomes a reality of the society's evils. I use my music to make people happy, to give them good advice; also in saying things that will benefit our country, Nigeria.

For instance, in 1960 I composed a song called "*Anyi bu off*" (We are one); I was telling all Nigerians to unite. I also did another one in 1962 titled "*Ezigbo Omume*" (Good behaviour). It is the same thing as "War Against indiscipline" isn't it? Whatever one sows, one shall reap it, be a good citizen and do your work well so that you will be honoured either on this earth or in the heaven above. Another one is "*Ogo di mkpa*" (Help is important). To help someone is very good. A good person never forgets the one who helped him. Help your fellow man so that God will help you.

Another song is "*Agbal'aka ne-azo ani, onye a naekonye.*" If you were not armed with seeds, it is useless to go on with land dispute - or if you had no yam-seedlings during planting season and you go on disputing for land, you will discover that your rival with yam seedlings will go on planting and consolidating his claim. This track was misinterpreted by many people who thought that I had a land dispute with somebody. That was incorrect, I was actually predicting what will happen if the government and the people stay idle and shout for a change in the country's economy and social well-being. If they are not ready to fight for the country's low economy, let them not do it, because any empty-handed attempt will cause the intervention of out-bidders. Before a farmer grows his yams he will first get hold of a plot of land and money for the labourers. Still, another song is "*Onu kwulu njo giekwu mma.*" Those who condemn past rulers and administrators will eventually be the ones to praise them. I have seen that music has now been a forum through which bad behaviour is preached against, and also advice and praise are being given. As they say, a hungry man is an angry man. Hunger doesn't let the hungry to see clearly and if he doesn't see clearly, he can't perform any work well. So the most vital thing now is food. It is much hunger and starvation that brought about indiscipline in the society. Again, unemployment - this creates its own problems. It is not everybody that can afford to train his or her child (children) up to secondary school level, to high education level or to university. The number of school leavers is so great these days. There is no work in the country. When you add the present unemployed people to those that graduated years before, still unemployed, you can see a whole lot of problem for the nation.

Musicians are trying very much. They are saying what should be done, and will continue saying it, until they are done.

There are many ways through which all these could be said in music. It is not many people that like what is being said. Some people buy a record because it is the type they like; some buy it because they consider it as a forum which tells them what to do in a particular situation. So, there are a thousand and one ways of reducing the problems facing our country through music, the only thing that remains is this: the person you talked to, did it enter his ears; what did he do with it after hearing? I won't say we musicians have done enough. Our modern musicians are more on pop, disco-rock music. They lay more emphasis on love music than on the ones that will help remedy the situation in the country. Musicians like Jim Reeves and others are playing the kind of music which their country needs for making amendments but our musicians are just copying those musicians who play only for the pleasure of it and for people's enjoyment, forgetting that we still need solutions to our problems. They never play what will be useful to our people, but play for other people's benefit. All of these have accounted for bad morals in the youths. Students go to disco parties and mess around; they develop all sorts of bad manners. When it comes to traditional and cultural display, they become incapable. Our people love foreign music more than their own type of music. Many people buy Congo music, Ghanaian music, European music, etc., which they don't understand, forgetting that we have traditional music which contains essential messages for the development of the country's economy and social well-being. When they buy these foreign types of music, they do not know that they are helping to promote those foreign musicians and their music while theirs always stay in the background. But these people never buy records produced by our musicians.

    I am a composer, arranger, director, player and singer. Why do I always mention God in my music? What is the work of 'Chi' in my style of music? Like in Paulson Kalu's "*Okwu dill Chukw,*" backed by my band, the position and place of God is very clear to me. In "*Chi nwe Okwu,*" my own album, I explained that some people use their position to abuse other people, some abuse their fellow human beings and wish the deaths of their relations. Those who are well-placed in life should not abuse the underprivileged because they themselves are incapable of controlling tomorrow. The underprivileged are not in the position they are in by their own making, so also the privileged. God is the sole maker of everybody, everything.

    I am the Chairman of PMAN (performing Musicians Association of Nigeria) Anambra State, and Chairman of Eastern Zone. Eastern Zone comprises Anambra, Imo, Rivers and Cross River.

I made no promise to myself which I thought ought to be fulfilled but 1 only asked God for a favour. When I left my work and went into music, my father disagreed with me on my decision as I said earlier on, but he later gave consent after my uncle's persuasion. My only promise was to my father confirming that I was not going to become a reckless or wayward musician. My appeal to God and the favours which I asked from God have since been fulfilled. I married in good time. My first wife from Abeokuta whom I married in 1960 is still living with me; the second wife in 1967; the third in 1972 and the fourth in 1979. I have both male and female children but my only regret is that some of them are dead. Some are in higher institutions of learning, in colleges, few in primary school and some overseas. I am the first Igbo musician in Nigeria to win "a language Gold disc" with my record titled "Osadebe 75;" I am the first Nigerian musician to win the mighty platinum plate and the two gold discs in one award.

I thank God that as at this day all my family, relations etc are all well. My immediate uncle lives with me and no matter the situation, whatever happens, we certainly find some *garri* to drink. I am not yet prepared to retire. I have got what I wanted in life; what I wanted from music. I am going to get another award from Polygram. It has something to do with national and world recognition. The award will come through the Federal Government. The Minister for Information, Social Development, Youths, Sports and Culture will be the presenter.

## Victor Uwaifo

When I was interviewed on BBC, London...I explained that my music is rich in African culture as demonstrated in the beat and lyrics. The fact that I use modern musical instruments to produce my sound has not altered the basic characteristics of my music; otherwise, we might as well argue that a historian writing ancient history with modem tools, like a Parker pen and paper, is a farce. The tools he uses to write his history will not alter the facts of his book.

I often give free shows and donations in aid of the suffering and towards the advancement of human culture. For instance, I have played at many schools and colleges, health organizations and institutions for the blind and deaf.

I was born in 1941 at Benin-City, the ancient capital of Benin Empire in Nigeria. I was born at home since in those days mothers could deliver anywhere. In fact, my father had five wives, or as they say in our tradition, he had five doors. We were a family of thirteen and I was the last one. My father was a policeman and he rose to the rank of Sergeant, which was very rare at that time. When he retired, he became a building contractor.

My father was a strict and disciplined man, no wonder, being a policeman. From when I was about two years old he used to call me to come and dance to Spanish tunes and rumbas on gramophone records. As I recall, they were called G.V. Records and were numbered one, two, three and so on. I used to dance so well that it became an everyday thing; whenever a stranger came they would put on the gramophone for me to dance to and give me "a dash" of the British colonial coin which was one penny. My whole family was musically inclined and everyone played one kind of instrument or another. My father used to play accordion and my mother was a very beautiful singer who used to take the lead in Church. All my other brothers grew in that atmosphere and two of them are still musicians. Among others are Eddy Uwaifo, an automobile engineer; S.O. Uwaifo, a high court Judge; G.O. Uwaifo, a lawyer; Amua Uwaifo, a pensioneer - senior customs officer; Oseni Uwaifo, a medical officer; Julie, a nursing sister; Clara, trained teacher; Esther, graduate teacher; Clement, musician; Douglas, art director; Christopher, musician.

At about seven years old, I tried my hands at

making cassava graters for making *garri* (made by punching holes in a metal sheet; rather like a cheese grater). My elder brothers used to do this and I joined them and became very good at it and used to make patterns and designs which buyers liked. This was the first sign of my talent in art. What I hated most was telling stories, I just couldn't relate stories. It's quite really surprising that when I hit the limelight and found myself in a position to exploit Binin folk-stories they all came back to me subconsciously.

During those days, I used to go around to the palm-wine guitarist downtown. Each time they struck a chord, it vibrated through my body and I thought I should be able to play that sort of a thing too. The most famous of these guitarists in Benin was We-We, who had been a soldier during the Second World War. So, I made a crude guitar myself with high tension wires for strings and bicycle spokes for frets; but I started it all wrong as I tuned the guitar to give me the notation (i.e. tuned to a chord).

I did this for almost a year trying a 'few songs' as I thought I was doing alright. Then, one day, I went to a palm-wine bar and borrowed a guitar to show-off with, when to my amazement I couldn't play. I asked why I couldn't play it and tried to alter the tuning but the man couldn't allow me as he told me his tuning the correct and universal way. I didn't believe him and tried two other guitarists, but they were the same. Finally, I begged one of them to teach me to tune the guitar the proper way and he said unless I bought him a jug of palm-wine. Fortunately; I had six pence on me so I bought him a jug and he taught me to tune-up and play some simple tunes.

It was after this that I found that my home-made guitar was very inferior, so I decided to buy one for myself but it was difficult as I didn't know how to put it to my father, for he would never agree. The idea that I was going to buy a guitar would be a crime; so, I decided to go somewhere and work to earn money as a labourer. Nearby, they were building a new house and for seven days during the holidays I went there. I knew that my father being a man of dignity would be sad to hear that I needed to raise money in the same street; as if our family didn't have enough money. But I earned my one guinea and bought a second-hand guitar.

I had a better opportunity to learn how to play the guitar when I left primary school and was waiting for my Common Entrance Examination results. My father had a contract at Benin and he asked me to go there and take stock of materials as a clerk. Fortunately, at the place I was staying, there was a guitarist. Well, I had my guitar and he had his, so we used to jam-up. Sometimes, he told me to play "competee" (competition) with him and other times he would tell me to play the background and he would take the solo. He was very good at the guitar and his job was a driver of a tipper truck.

I went to secondary school in Benin but after two years, I lost my father and so my brother in Lagos asked me to join him. I got admission to St. Gregory's College which was very rare as St. Gregory's and King's College were the most exclusive schools in Nigeria. To get into these schools you either had to be extremely intelligent or belong to the rich. They gave me a test and I did very well, then later the school learnt that I was an athlete and musician in the making so I became an asset to the school.

It was during my time there that the whole revolution of school pop bands started. A school band was formed to keep me within the gates and another was formed at King's College with Segun Bucknor as the leader. We used to have Saturday night out either in our school or theirs and we played pop music like Cliff Richards and Elvis Presley and also highlife music of the E.T. Mensah's type. Later, similar bands were formed in other schools. In fact, I used to see E.T. Mensah and his Tempos play whenever they were in Benin and the year I lost my father I went to see their guitarist, Dizzy Acquaye, to put me through a few chords. I had a guitar book my brother had bought me but I didn't understand the chords, instead of illustrating the full neck of the guitar, they only drew the frets; Dizzy helped me. Fortunately, at St.

Gregory's we had a music tutor so I obtained perfect knowledge of the rudiments of music thus, I headed the school band. It was during these school days that I spent nine months with Victor Olaiya's 'All Stars,' playing during the holidays and weekends.

In 1962, after I left school, I had the opportunity to go to the College of Technology at Yaba in Lagos to study Graphic Art. While there I won a scholarship for some paintings I did and this gave me time for my music, for I didn't have to worry so much about money as I had enough to live by.

I joined E.C. Arinze at Kakadu Night Club, whose band was very versatile and played every kind of music. In those days, you weren't recognized as a band leader unless you could play waltz, quick-steps, rumbas, highlife and everything. Musicians then were better as it was like going through a secondary school doing all subjects instead of majoring in one and having no knowledge of other subjects.

In E.C. Arinze's band I had two contemporaries who were strikingly talented too. Eddy Okonta, who described me as a combination of many dynamic elements -an enigma; and Etim Udoh, a brilliant nutcase of an alto player. I earned the nick-name "muscle-man" in E.C. Arinze's band.

Our association (Eddy and I) blossomed into a business partnership in the middle sixties when I went on a recording date to what used to be called "Phillips Studio." That was the birth of the "Pick-Ups," we later recorded for Jofabro.

I was at Yaba College of Technology for three years and then I joined the Nigerian Television Service as a Graphic Artist and after two years, I formed the 'Melody Maestros' in 1965. While at the television studio, I had a trio on a programme called "The Minstrel Programme." At first, I was playing folksong and highlife from Benin on my own. Later, it became a trio with bass guitar and congas added. It was very popular. I was earning very well at the television as I was on scale "C" ... So I was able to save and buy instruments (I recall that upon leaving school we had formed a group called the Central Modinaires).

We rehearsed at home and made a record for Phillips in 1965 called "*Siwo-Siwo*" This was a popular alright but the second one "*Joromi*" came as a reassurance that a new sound was born. After this, I had another successful single called "Guitar-Boy." "*Joromi*" was so popular that Phillips presented me with a gold disc for one hundred thousand copies of it sold in one year. I was crowned "Sir Victor Uwaifo" by the students at the University of Nigeria, Nsukka. Before, there had been other musicians who lived by different titles, like "Cardinal" -Rex Jim Lawson. So, the students said 1 was a knight of music. I transposed the colours of '*Akwete*' cloth, a hand-woven cloth made in Eastern Nigeria, a very beautiful cloth, creating a moving rhythm of colours. When I interpreted this, it gave the sound which I later called "*Akwete*." I developed the "Shadow" which was link between "*Akwete*" and the "Twist."

I first derived this dance the 'Shadow' as I stood one day and looked at my shadow and likened it to death, man's inevitable destiny. I thought that every movement in a dance casts a peculiar shadow on the ground. As the dance comes to an end, the shadow cast by the movement of the dancer fades away, just as the body of a man perishes as he dies. To catch your own shadow is impossible, so out of this, I created patterns and dance-steps.

Then I came up with a new idea - *Ekassa*. In fact, I wouldn't say I created *Ekassa* as it was already there as an indigenous dance of Benin. It was a royal danced done during the coronation of a new king.

In 1974, 1 created *Sasakosa*, coined from the name of *Sasako*, who used to sing in a popular way to warn (the king-in-hiding) that there was danger around. *Sasako* was the king's orderly and played this outstanding role to protect the Oba of Benin from the "British avengers," who executed the Binin Massacre as a vendetta. But "*Gioromi*" or "*Joromi*," drawn from Binin folktale, was so popular that it gave its name to the patterned weaving on West African *Joromi* shirts. I am married; I have children by my marriage. 1 met my wife in Accra, Ghana, in 1966 at the house of her brother, Mr. Joe Fosu, who was my friend. That generated many a visit to Ghana over the years. I recall cruising to Ghana in my citron safari to see my favourite girl (now Lady Adelaide Uwaifo, fondly called "Mama"). She is now a career woman, a lawyer by profession, practising in Binin-City, Nigeria. She studied at the University of Lagos from 1973 to 1976 and was called to the Bar in 1977. We married first by native law and custom in 1972, then in the Church - The Holy Cross Cathedral in Benin City in 1973. It was a colourful wedding with a strong representation from the musician association of Nigeria. A Bishop and four Reverend Fathers officiated. To grace the occasion, the first Bishop of Benin, rather old now -Bishop Kelly- was there to observe things.

I was commissioned by the Federal Government to represent Nigeria in 1969 at the All African Festival of Arts held in Algiers (Algeria) in 1970; also, I represented Nigeria at the Expo 70, Japan; and in 1973 USSR; and featured prominently in Festac '77 in Lagos. I was the first Nigerian musician to perform at the UN Assembly, New York in 1970. The standing ovation I received after each performance showed my musical excellence and prominence. My contribution to music has earned me so many awards: "Honorary Doctor of Music certificate" by the Edo Club, Benin; "Decoration" by the Sigma Club (of Ibadan University); the Grand Order of Havana (G.O.H); "Certificate of merit" by the Enugu Sports Club as the musician-of-the-year 1981.

I can also claim to be a distinguished personality because I was listed in the Africa's 'Who is Who' encyclopaedia, 1982 edition. I am a member of the performing Whites Sites of Great Britain and Sachem of France. I am the governor of PMAN (Performing Musician Association of Nigeria), Bendel State Branch. I am a great instrumentalist; 1 play guitar, flute, saxophone, piano and other instruments. 1 am the humble owner of 'Joromy Recording and Television Studio' in Benin City; the first of its kind in Africa. I feel I have made outstanding contributions through the promotion of our arts and culture with my music all over the world. For this reason, the former President of the Federal Republic of Nigeria, Alhaji

Shehu Shagari conferred on me a National Honours Award of Member of the Order of Niger (MON) on 1, October 1982.

## Melvin Ukachi

Melvin Ukachi was the leader of the "first wonder-boys" of Nigeria's 'pop' music called "*ofege.*"

> In our first album, 'Try and Love,' there was a message in the lyrics ... telling the people to try and love their neighbours. You may say that the message came from a child's mind since we were still at secondary school, at St. Gregory's College, Lagos." "*Monomono* rhythms influenced us." "I now play something like pop-disco, calypso highlife ... there is need for us to go back to our roots.
>
> A musician needs not ask questions with his lyrics if he wants to lead the society positively, he should recommend answers and solutions.
>
> Born on 9 April 1958, from childhood, I picked up interest in music. I played with things like tin-cans, empty tins of milk, ash-trays, even the normal trays used for serving drinks. My parents and relations wanted me to do engineering which I had very good potentials for because I was very good at fixing and unfitting things. I tried to do what was expected of me but later found out that inwardly, I couldn't go on. Then I followed my own mind and landed in this position.
>  I started secondary school in 1971 at St. Gregory's College in Lagos. I did not have much contact with musical instruments until around the age of 14, may be because I was then a junior student. When I got to senior class, my friends and I, who were interested in music, were allowed to use a band's instruments. We were allowed into the rehearsal rooms and were given access to the instruments. We never knew how to play guitar at all. They started teaching us how to play the guitar. One

of the band members started teaching us the basic chords of the instruments. After that, when we got used to the instruments, we used to play in the evenings, instead of going to play games; we gathered in one place and performed. Our group was named "*Ofege*" and the pioneering instrumentalists comprised Paul Olaje, one other student and I, (basically three of us) on drums, the bass and guitar. We usually went to the lawn tennis court to play (inside the school premises). One day, we thought that since we were soon going to complete our secondary school education, we could make a disc. We never knew what recording was all about but, I wanted us to do some recording so that the recording company could give us a copy each after recording which we could take home. It never crossed my mind that it would be so popular. That was how it started.

Looking at it, I had no real musical training in handling any of the instruments. I had no formal training. It just happened that a musician who was interested in our school band used to borrow our guitar. To pay us back, he decided to teach us how to play and handle the instruments.

We did not copy or go after anybody, but as our musical model, the fact was that if there was a type of musical trend going on, people would be induced to it, even if you were not copying it, you would be playing a rhythm which would lead to or be similar to that one. The reigning band then was *Monomono* style. There was pop music also but we felt differently and played differently, but ours was more commercial. It was a sort of luck, if we had followed the style of the school band; the result would not have been the same. So, all in all, it was the *Monomono* that inspired us.

Following our success, there were usually questions from our fans and critics: what was the first number you made as a group in *Ofege*? Or was there any hardships or something like that? In other words, did the recording companies instantly realize that you had good qualities or did you have to pull your weight to convince them that you were full of potentials before they agreed to record your music?

We took the initiative and went to the recording companies. Before then, the senior school band had gone to these companies. The music they played then was not considered commercial enough to make a market. So, when we went, the company representatives asked "why don't you people go back to school, we've had you before, your senior band had been here before and we didn't like their presentation."

We did all we could to convince them but they were biased. Whatever we played, the company never listened to. So, we left that place in frustration. We never went back to them. Instead, we started looking out for another recording company.

I discovered then that EMI was in Apapa. We went there and met one Obiorah who interviewed us. He gave us a chance on a certain condition. We were auditioned; the managing director, one Mr. Simons, was there, and we never knew what was going on in the control room, or how excited the company was. We were just enjoying our own music. We were surprised when after the whole thing we were asked to sign a contract on the spot. From then on, we made other records and in later years, I even forgot about all that we suffered in the early years to record the first album.

The first number we made as a group in *Ofege* was 'Try and Love.' Another big surprise we had in those days was that when we opened a newspaper, we saw our picture, an article and comment about us.

I was in the lead, I was everything; the composer, the arranger, the band-leader, the producer or something of that sort. I never discarded any member's creativity. We usually compared our stuff and chose the ones to play. I sometimes acted as a by-stander, piloting the whole affairs indirectly without causing internal jealousy. That was why we never had any misunderstanding. This went on smoothly.

In our first album, 'Try and Love', there was a message conveyed to the people in the lyrics. In the album, we were telling the people to try and love their neighbours, although you may say that the message came from a child's mind. We never really had deep appreciation of what we were doing then. It never meant anything to us at that time. It was something like the ingenuity of the song which others recognized. It was like a child saying something meaningful while not realizing himself that he was saying something meaningful.

After the first album "Try and Love" came the second, "Last of the Origins," (both at EMI). We then rearranged ourselves and our style and after, went to Polygram to record. The album was "Higher Plain Bridges" (HPB). The 4th still in Polygram was "How do you feel."

Sometime in 1979, 1 came back to EMI. That was when I started playing solo. I made some friends; J. Robinson and one Frank and we made the 5th album called "Where are my people." It was a call to brotherhood because, it is known, especially in our area (Igboland), that the Igboman *"no know him brother, instead of helping him brother, e go help another person."* It was from my experience; I had a series of rough deals. Such rough deals led me to compose that song. Even my own people, my family, my uncles, my relations, my town chief and townspeople would rather show-off their riches in what interests their exhibitionism, I mean things in which they can't have any real benefit, than help their son to get to the heights. They preferred displaying their wealth for people's notice, without any intention of rendering any help or support, of any kind, to their own people who are talented enough to produce some artistic work.

We made the first four numbers as a group, one as a semi-group because the group then comprised only MSF (Melvin, Shoga and Frank). The next album was a "Solo" in about 1982 called "Revolution."

*Ofege* virtually exists even up till today. We can spring up again at any time. We know how to get ourselves together if need be. What dispersed us was the fact that some wanted to go out for further studies, some wanted to do other business but we have continued to keep in touch.

All the time, I knew my mind. I had a different

aspiration; that has been to stay on with music because even with all the degrees like PhD, MA, BA, BSc., one was bound to look for a job after acquiring them. For me, there was no need to look for work to do. There is always some work for a musician. It comes from both left and right. So, in the near future, we might have the *Ofege* back on the musical scene.

Let's talk about our revolution. In our albums, the messages we were trying to put across can be summed up in our goals. Now here, we are living in another man's system (the Whiteman's), not in our own. We, as Africans, belong to a different race. I just realized that we cannot survive in a foreign system because we can never claim that system is ours. We have to develop our own and a good one. You can imagine how it will be if we evolve something new from it. Five hundred years ago, the Whiteman's culture was barbaric, but they evolved something new.

Music helps to develop a society; it educates, informs and entertains. Don't you see that music plays an important role in the reformation of our culture? If we can revive our culture, while developing our culture musically, our society will grow up in several dimensions.

I don't see the relevance of asking questions with music. It is better to be positive; just get out the answer to a question. That is what really matters; find a solution, the way, or the path towards solving problems. Point the best possible way to get our country out of the mess that it is now. Why ask Nigeria which way? You don't know, I don't know so we get no answer. The answer to "Which way Nigeria" is a "revolution." That's the only way out; to turn round and do something for ourselves, think out something for the better.

Nigeria is an under-developed society. She is trying hard to develop, but we have problems keeping us back. Social problems like tribalism, though that has softened up. Quick money is responsible for all the set-backs and danger. When somebody in the office wants to make quick cash, he becomes inefficient, becomes more interested in kick-backs.

Hunger, poverty or whatever, are bye-products of the individual enrichment craze as well as mal-administration. One hopes the new revolutionary trend in administration will last and stay. I see the possibility of music being used as a forum to try and solve or lessen our problems? I feel it is a good thing to exploit music for patriotism and nationalism. Although I am not aware of what others might do with their music, mine is to help and evolve a new order to solve our problems. My view is that other artists should do the same because, even in social development programmes, governments look for music to highlight the occasion. I believe no human being can do without music.

I play something like pop-disco-calypso-highlife. There is a need for us, Nigerians, to go back to our roots, to our culture. Indeed, now I know what we can call our cultural and traditional music. I play a different kind of music which is a combination of music, each different from the other. I see my style as a forum from where impact could be made on the society considering the drive towards self-awareness; it is like prophecy. Series of governments have hammered and are still hammering on self-awareness. Artists are doing the same thing as the government; artists are even prophesying to the people and they are bound to succeed.

I don't criticize the society, I want to lead them. 1 also make sure that my music is commercial enough to be circulated.

Most of our musicians are just copying one another. They are not being original. They are just loitering about, just orienting towards the commercial aspect. They don't have enough messages in their music. It is only a few -quite a few that give us some messages. The only way to remedy things is through evolution, evolution of the Black Man. We don't need any other message now because time is running out. The Whites are coming back very soon. It might be in fifty years time, it might be sixty but I guarantee everybody that unless we start evolving, we might not be free for more than one hundred years from now. As I said earlier on, if there is anything like financial dream, I would say that 1 am alright but my major dream now is to become an industrialist. I am sort of a mixed-up being. Artistically, I have capabilities. Scientifically, I am up to it. Whenever an album brings money to me, I use the money to set up some other things.

The only disturbance I encounter is from people, who don't know what they want; all in all, no setbacks whatsoever. I hope that our people will get developed, understand more about life, and the full meaning of life.

## Alhaji Dan Maraya

Before Alhaji Dan Maraya blows his own trumpet, it is important for the following background to be established. The interview with Alhaji Dan Maraya was held from 19 September, 1976, for several days, in his home at Jos. Upon our first meeting at Jos in 1973, we became friends.

In 1978 when I was invited to Cardiff in Wales by the Nigerian Union in UK, during a Nigerian Week of symposia, lectures and cultural festival, Alhaji Dan Maraya was also invited. He was to do his great *Kuntigi* show. I was invited to give a lecture on "the role of drama in education in Nigeria." Unfortunately, Alhaji Dan Maraya went to UK ahead of me and performed before I arrived.

His artistic communication was fantastic, according to reports, but it was not very effective. Mr. Geoffrey Axworthy, Director of Theatre at the University College, Sherman, rescheduled a repeat performance for him and waited for me. Upon arrival, Geoffrey, my own old teacher, requested me to be Dan Maraya's compere. He described Dan Maraya as Africa's George Fomby.

I arranged a triangular meeting involving Alhaji Gwaska (also of Plateau State in Nigeria), Dan Maraya and myself. This meeting was very crucial because I could not rely confidently on my Hausa when it comes to Dan Maraya's poetic, satirical lyrics in Hausa. Alhaji Gwaska (a one time Secretary of Local Government Education at Jos and later political adviser to Governor Solomon Lar) was happy to be involved. He translated all I needed for my interpretation.

I represented Alhaji Dan Maraya and his *Kuntigi* to the Euro-Pan African audience at which the Nigerian Acting High commissioner in London, Mr. Monu, was present. For this repeat show, which I was the compere, Alhaji Dan Maraya received a standing ovation.

The Plateau women studying at Cardiff held a special "*tuo*

*shinkafa*-okra soup" party in my honour. The dailies came out with a feature on Alhaji Dan maraya. BBC was already familiar with that name; BBC in London sent a producer to Cardiff to invite me down to their interview-programme "Arts and Africa" by Florence Akst. That programme featured my latest album "Late Nite Husband" and my published play, *The Old Masters*. Of course, I was not new to BBC African Overseas Service, having been their guest in 1973 on "Calling Nigeria." Thus, I considered myself artistically qualified to project the *Kuntigi* solo artist, Alhaji Dan Maraya. The rapport between his *Kuntigi* song-texts and those of highlife qualifies him herein to make autobiographical statements.

> My real name is Adamu Mohammed; Adamu is the name of my grandfather. I lost both my mother and father rather early. I was too young when they died to even recognize them. I suppose I was born around 1946 at Bukuru near Jos. My parents were natives of Sokoto.
> My father was a royal musician. He played "*Kotso*" music. He played mainly for chiefs as a praise-singer.
> I attended a Koranic School at the age of six at Bukuru for one and a half years. I was compelled to attend a formal elementary school for one year only because I was not interested. But when I turned eight and a half years, I was interested in following the foot-steps of my father as a musician, thus I started *Kotso* music.
> The district head of Bukuru, Alhaji Muhammadu Sarikin Bukuru became my guardian and treated me warmly. Since my father was his royal musician, upon his death, the Sarikin took over responsibilities for my training. A woman - a baby nurse was charged with my up-bringing.
> Sarikin adopted me; but among the Hausas, adoption does not establish legal relationship, it amounts only to emotional relationship which brooks no bond and legal commitment. Thus, although the Sarikin's (or chief) intention was to give me real education, my own inclination destroyed it.
> I loved foot-balling. I always had a small tennis-ball in my pocket to play around.

For music-making, I was mainly influenced by a lady musician named Mamu. She was a *kotso*-player backed by her two grand-children who were drummers. I virtually became Mamu's disciple. But Mamu played only for chiefs while her grandchildren played in popular places, like the market.

It was on one of such market-place-shows that both I and Mamu's grandchildren met, sharing musical showbiz interest. They introduced me to Mamu, later.

Together with them I made music a transit show in Bukuru-Jos taxi. We all left later to Bauchi. Mamu's grandsons played *Kuntigi* but they refused to teach me, fearing that I might spoil the instrument. Later, they granted me a chance and I played well, so we all left for Maiduguri.

Before I discuss my experience at Maiduguri, let me talk about Kano, who was already making *Kuntigi* music. I had apprenticed myself to him to understudy him. I was doing so well that Kano became afraid and jealous of my potentials in *Kuntigi* music. Occasionally, he would destroy his *Kuntigi* guitar to make it impossible for me to learn. His attitude provoked me a lot and became a challenge to my curiosity and interest. Thus, I tried my hand at improvising the *Kuntigi* guitar, using a match-box. I coined the string from a horse's flywhisk tied on to special "*suya*-sticks."

Thus, before my trip to Maiduguri with Mamu's grandsons, I was already on my way to building a solid *Kuntigi* guitar for my shows.

At Maiduguri, we played commercial *Kotso* for two years to make money to finance a Mecca trip for Hajj. One day, I picked up an empty "fish-can" with which 1 built my own real *Kuntigi* to replace the improvised one.

At the end of two years, Mamu began being cold towards me, he treated me no longer as a son and ended up giving me only three (3) shillings as my allowance from the proceeds of two years, so we parted.

I sought asylum in the place of Mallam Idris and played *Kuntigi* for apprentice drivers. I was a strolling entertainer, trekking the roads and performing at dead-ends or where mammy-wagons (trailers) broke down and had drivers and motor-boys guarding the loaded trucks. I also worked as a "tout" loading mammy-wagons or commercial vehicles. I left Maiduguri in about 1962.

My main spectators were still drivers, their apprentices and touts. I arrived at Zaria and from Zaria to Kaduna.

The first media executive to scout me was Adamu Gumel (of blessed memory). He was a broadcaster of the Nigerian Broadcasting Corporation. He got me to perform for the radio. How much I was paid was not as important then. My enthusiasm and excitement surpassed the urge for fees.

My show attracted patrons who began donating in kind and cash to keep me. By now, Broadcasting Corporation of Northern Nigeria (BCNN) has been opened. Television was strange then.

I showed up at the TV station uninvited at Kaduna. Yusuf Laden was amused but became interested when he discovered that I was a talented musician. At that time, I was unable to differentiate live shows on TV from recorded ones. The subjects of my song-texts concentrated on "*Karomata*" (apprentice drivers); "*Dan Omolanke*" (truck pushers); "*Dan Ladi*" (those who loaded lorries).

My song-texts were satirical; the messages underlined the plight and activities of these fellows. Even while singing, I impersonated their characters to give better interpretation of their experiences in poverty and suffering. I gained greater recognition by viewers.

Alhaji Sani Kotangora, the head of the BCNN then was won over by my talents and my lowly birth as an orphan. He offered me food, clothing and shelter. I spent only two months with Alhaji Kotangora. My contact with the Nigerian Broadcasting Corporation (NBC) and BCNN (Broadcasting Corporation of Northern Nigeria) had brought a new interest in my work. My fans grew because I was well publicized. My satirical tit-bits became popular and were demanded. Yes the demand for my "*Karanmatu* songs" grew.

My popularity attracted the interest of Miners (Tin Miners in Plateau State of Nigeria). I was invited to make music at Barkin Ladi and at Sabon Gida Danyanya tin-mines. I noticed that minefield-workers were interested in gambling. I wrote songs about gambling to entertain them. My song about labourers is related to gambles. It has since been converted to commercial discs.

I must admit that Rock City Bar in Jos will remain a venue important to the development of my talents and my artistry. Influenced by Indian drums and Indian films, I began accompanying myself with the drums. The audience began buying the idea when Audu Yaron Goje came into the scene. He was a very popular goje musician.

I accompanied Audu Yaron Goje with my new improvised Indian drums. The audience jumped for the combination. As a result, a trip was made to Kano. It was then at Kano that I made my first disc waxing at Tabansi Records. I played the drums and for live shows, I did acrobatics; dancing with four women in my showbiz.

Although I entertained politicians, I refused to be a partisan. I remained an artist uninfluenced by politicians. The late Sir Ahmadu Bello, the Sardauna of Sokoto, was so fond of me that I became his regular entertainer any time he visited Jos. Upon his death, I wrote a dirge about him, which was waxed on EMI. Ibrahim Aliyu, an assistant producer of Nigerian Languages Programme of NBC Jos has been of immense help to me.

During the Nigerian Civil War, I awakened the interest of youths to join the army to keep Nigeria united. My songs were so nationalistic in their ideas that I became an important entertainer of the Federal troops at the war-front or at the army base. One of such entertainments took me to Abakaliki in the defunct Eastern Nigeria.

I was in so much demand for the entertainment of the fighting troops that in one occasion, I had to send a disappointing telegram to Commander Joda who needed me to entertain some troops. The telegram read:

*Your telegram received. Thanks.*
*Gone to Awka to entertain 20 BN*
*on request. Aliyu Doma fully*
*informed to inform you.*

I was really admired by the Army. My contributions during the civil war were highly appreciated. I had enough facilities for my "job" -land rovers, body-guards, etc.

Some commanders presented me to the troops as "the man whose weapon was his *Kuntigi"* and added, "the only way to reciprocate was to use the gun to bring peace and unity."

When the NBC, Enugu was recaptured, I was the first to entertain on that medium.

My skill and talents have been adequately rewarded. I have virtually covered the whole world, representing Nigeria as a cultural entertainer -New York, United Nations, London, Paris, Tokyo, other African States, name it. No festival has passed without my presence, including Festac '77. I have also been bestowed with Nigerian National Honors -MON (Member of the Order of the Niger).

I am overwhelmed by organizations inviting me for jingles. Researchers in the universities also invite me to contribute my practical knowledge to their work. My experience and my work have become subjects of research and degree essays in the universities for a number of years. I can say that I am not only an entertainer now but even a consultant.

## Mike Ejeagha

*"Gentleman" Mike Ejeagha - Igbo folklore-highlife Architect.*

I am taking the initiative to offer about three hundred tapes of my field work on Igbo folklore music to the National Archives to help researchers who may be interested.

Love songs based on boy-meets-girl or man-meets-woman cannot help this country in this period when we are still trying to grow into nationhood.

As musicians, we should plead with our leaders not to continue to split this country for their own personal gains, or pretend to unite it for their own personal gains.

The animal characters in my "*Akuk-n'egwu*" are human beings in the society. My aim is not to make a caricature of politicians, community leaders and laymen, my aim is to highlight the morals in my folklore music in order to change this society to citizens who love one another, who are hard-working and honest, who are no 'cheaters' but their brothers keepers.

When I was in elementary school, I was a member of St. Patrick's choir. I joined some other children in playing traditional music.

It was then I met one Cyprian Ozochiawa, a native of Oye near Udi area in Anambra State of Nigeria. He was a barber and guitarist.

After my elementary education, I went to him in 1950 and apprenticed myself to him in order to become a barber and guitarist. In 1955, I began running my own barber's workshop.

I also did "part-time" with my guitar. Thus in 1963, I organized a small group of three. I made contact with Nigerian Broadcasting Service at Enugu and initiated a programme called "Guitar-Playtime." The brain behind me then was a broadcaster named Joe Atuona who was later a popular national newscaster. He was the controller of programmes in NBS Enugu at the time that my programme took-off under producers named Egbuna Obidike and Lawrence Emeka.

Between 1962 and 1963, I produced my first single under C.T. Onyekwelu. The titles of my songs (which were in Igbo language) were "Coaliary Massacre" and "Unfortunate Woman." The number, "Coaliary Massacre" is a true story of the massacre of coal miners by the colonial police simply because they went on strike for better conditions of service. The other number, "Unfortunate Woman" was based on a terrible incident in which a prison wardress, Mrs.

Onyia, was strangled to death in Enugu Prisons.

I was brought up in a Christian home. The idea of playing in brothels (or hotels) was, to me, morally objectionable. Apart from my barber's workshop, I was also running a bookshop. Since I still needed to develop my arts as a guitarist, it remained an important hobby for me.

Earlier on in 1960, one Joseph Ogbu, a hotelier (and also a guitarist himself) approached me to replace a guitarist in his band resident for his Paradise Hotel. The thought of contact with harlots and other immoral elements made it difficult for me to accept. Mr. Ogbu could not persuade me to accept until he met my mother for approval. She accepted and I accepted in respect of her intervention but it was on a "part-time" basis.

I usually arrived at Paradise Hotel at 8.30 p.m; we usually started playing dance music from 9.00 p.m. to 2.00 a.m. and I would be taken home immediately after.

Thus it was in 1960 that I decided to turn professional. In 1961, I produced an extended musical disc with the title "*Ofu Nwa Anaa.*" The lyrics were based on folklore. Between 1961 and 1963, I produced another musical disc, "Solomon's Wisdom." In October, 1964, I bargained and sold out my shop.

I bought my own musical instruments and played at the Dayspring Hotel at Enugu. Later, I moved to Eastern Star Hotel at Uwani, still in Enugu. Still I moved again to Freedom Hotel.

The first Nigerian *coup de'tat* took place in 1966 while I was still playing for Freedom Hotel; there was chaos everywhere.

I moved to Abakaliki and played for a while at the Premier Hotel there. Confusion increased following the coup and finally led to my abandoning my musical instruments to seek refuge elsewhere.

I already had my experience which was enriched by a switch-over from Guitar-Playtime to Igbo Drama (a play) at the NBC. I had also moved to Moonlight Orchestra at Asaba. I had done a number of programmes for East Central Broadcasting Service and during the war I did quite a number of shows for the Voice of Biafra.

After the war, I started playing at Green Virgin Hotel. The hotel's management later disqualified me because I couldn't play soul music. I didn't want to play Soul music because I knew that like Cha-cha, Twist and other imported rhythms, I was sure it would fade from the Nigerian musical scene sooner or later.

I preferred Ghana rhythms; there were definite similarities with our own music and in spite of the fact that I did not understand Ghanaian languages, Ghanaian music had a great influence on me. It encouraged me to stick to my own style and to stay with Igbo as my own music language. Some of the results of my decision are discs like "*Onye ndidi n'eli azu ukpo,*" "*Ofo malu onye ji ya*" and "*Omeka-Agu.*"

Walter Enuorah later initiated a TV-programme to expose my folklore music. The programme titled "*Akuko Na Egwu*" (or Tales and Traditional Dances) took off in 1972.

Based on "*Akuko Na Egwu*," the demand for my music by viewers increased to the extent that in 1983 the recording company which now handles my work confirmed, at the end of that year, that about 32,000 of my albums captioned "*Akuko Na Egwu*" had sold out. "*Udeze*" was another album released in early 1984.

Although my music is story-telling style, it is not that easy to get the messages upon first listening. I introduce proverbs and idioms into them so as to stimulate the mind of the listener. For instance, I employ what you may call riddles in a way: the tortoise asked his three sons to say how many times he can endure any offensive before he retaliates. The first could endure three, the second, two but the third said he could not stand it more than once so as to stop the enemy from destroying him. The third son thus won his father's heart with that answer.

It is obvious therefore that I use animals of the folklore world as parallels to human society. The incidents during the 1983 political campaigns and elections can be identified in the animals which are the characters within my musical tales.

My songs are loaded with meanings and messages, social, moral and political. These are evident in songs like "*Onye Ndidi N'eli Azu Ukpo*" (the patient man eats the fattest fish); "*Onye Nwe Onebe, Onye Enwegh Onebe*" (The rich is as needy as the poor - both still weep for something they lack) and "*Uwe Mgbede Ka Nma.*"

In my songs, I always wonder why brothers struggle over kingship or anything thereby even exterminating one another. Why are we in a hurry in everything? Why don't we take things easy? The palm-tree (ukwu) lasts longer than the swamp palm-tree (ngwo) because the former trickles its palm juice into the palm tapster's waiting container until it fills it up over a number of hours, but the latter pours out its juice like a waterfall and dies as a result of over-discharge because he who applies violence is swallowed by violence. We also preach that women, being the "weaker vessels" should be treated with greater understanding.

I believe that we must not cheat one another; that we must not give up until we know God's plans for us. We must not be ashamed of making efforts to better our fortune. Look at this moralistic story: a man went into a bush to commit suicide only to hear a plea from a cripple below the tree on which he wants to hang. "You may go ahead and commit your suicide," the cripple observed, "but please don't destroy me upon your crash. I am happy with what I am." The cripple thus rescued the man bent on self destruction because he was embarrassed by the cripple's desire for longer life. He gave up his suicide action and sneaked away from the bush.

A poor man can be transformed in a day into a wealthy man and vice versa. Our fortunes, our deeds and actions and our will dictate our situations. I don't believe that the wealthy is always cheating the poor. I believe that we should trust God and abide by His own time. I myself suffered a lot, never found anything easy, but today is definitely different from yesterday in my own fortune.

We live to help one another. Artists must help one another even financially because our rise to the top is difficult. We pass through very difficult times. I went for a recording once in Lagos. We were twenty sharing one-room with no facilities like water. Yet we were expected to do a good recording at the recording studio. Does good condition not promote good quality in the arts? Still we could not complain. We put in our best but I am sure that given a better condition, our best would have been better.

Love songs based on boy-meets-girl or man-meets-woman cannot help this country in this period when we are still trying to grow into nationhood. As musicians we should plead with our leaders not to continue to split this country for their own personal gains or pretend to unite it for their own personal gains.

After the war, in the early seventies, I decided to play deeper into our cultural and traditional music. I have listened to music from South Africa and Zaire and I found that there are some similarities in theirs and our own traditional music.

Just like a revolution which one man can plan and also carry out alone, I decided to draw folk music closer to modern instrument and make some impact. Fortunately, Anambra Broadcasting Corporation started the programme (*Akuko na egwu*) and I decided to produce some of my folklores on radio.

To collect the folklores, sometimes two of my musicians or all of us went to the village or farm-settlements to record folklores directly from the villagers. Of course, we had to go with tips like coconut, wine, kolanut and tobacco. When the famers returned from work in the evenings, we assembled later at night to listen to their folklores. As I said earlier on, we recorded them.

Back at Enugu, I adapt all the original stories and set them to my kind of music and rhythms. It is important to give credit to farm-settlements and villages like Agu-Ngena, Ekpele, Nsukka, Anam, Owa, etc.

Now that I have seen the impact folklores have already made, I have decided to make the tapes of these stories as many as possible and make an index of them and send them to national archives for preservation so that if any one wants to write about them, it will be easier to reach them through the archives. I know that in one or two decade to come, the sources of these folklores may dry up; already, the sources are becoming urbanized thus losing their wealth of folk stories.

Incidentally, the more the sources loose what they have, the more the cities need a recreation of folklores as evident in their interest in my productivities and creativities. My fans include prominent people in the society who send congratulatory messages to me, some of them even telling me stories about their childhood.

The presentation of the tapes of collected folklores to the National Archives will become my own personal contribution in the preservation of our culture -and I plan to continue to interpret folk stories into our modem music. In our future recordings of "*Akuko na egwu,*" I will introduce Western bass-guitar to our native *udu.*

If my fans are impressed, I will continue to use such technique instrumentally. In future, I may also introduce more local instruments so that outsiders may appreciate the integrity and quality of our culture because our native musical instruments are not inferior to the imported electronic ones.

I have got about 300 stories. The wit, wisdom and folklores which motivated my work came from my association with the elders and particularly with my mother who is very talented and helps me even now. Also, I owe my inspirations to my father and grandfather.

I was born in 1932. I am a native of Ime-Ezi Owa in Ezeagu Local Government Area. I schooled at St. Patrick's at Coal Camp in Enugu. I am now married and have some children. My greetings to Sonny Oti; he must keep up his efforts. Any information from me is always available to Sonny Oti without hesitation; he is really one of us.

## Celestine Obiakor

In spite of all these hot-sellers, what have I got? They play my record always and pay me nothing. But "*God dey, nothing pass-am.*" I am happy that people recognize what I have done to make this country a better place for all of us with my music.

At school, I attended a choir practice where we had Mallam Adamu as our choir-master. There I learnt how to play the guitar.

I am a native of Nekede near Owerri in Nigeria. I was born in 1932. My father is Obiakor Alozie. He was a carpenter. My mother is Florence Adaji.

It was my brother who brought Mallam Adamu to play in our house. The way he played it made me to try and play the guitar. I later was inspired to the extent of buying a guitar and. that was how 1 started having inspirations for music.

I started active music-making when I was working on a ship. I was in the marine business for seven years. Most passengers from Sierra Leone usually carried guitar. Our ship was based in Lagos. We travelled overseas a lot and I learned how to play this guitar from these people.

Then I came out of this ship work and joined one musician called Tommy Obeyi -a native of Benin in Nigeria. Steve Amechi from Onitsha and Tommy Obeyi took me because they said "if this man is taught how to play well, he will make it."

When I was in the ship business, I used to play guitar but when I went into orchestra under Tommy Obeyi, I was no longer playing any tune without knowing its meaning as I used to do in the ship.

I met Tommy Obeyi when I used to take my guitar to play in the streets. Tommy saw me and called me to play for him. He asked if I can read music and I said "no," so he taught me how to read music. He showed me the "chords" on the trumpet and the guitar and he gave me ideas.

I also played for Stephen Amechi and his Rhythm Stars. Stephen Amechi took me away from Tommy Obeyi because in Tommy's band, 1 was not given the chance to play to the best of my ability. I was not popularized.

When Stephen took me, I was one of his composition-makers. We made one titled "*Fada anugo olum*" and I feature prominently. He took me to places where I played for him unlike Tommy Obeyi. Stephen exposed me more than Tommy. Stephen took me to Enugu where we formed "The Leisure Garden Dance Band" in 1959. The band played at 21 Ogui Lane in Enugu. Then we played at Leisure Garden Hotel owned by Mr. Augustine Ekwensi.

Between 1959, 1960 and 1961, I played at Enugu but later left for Lagos. At Lagos, late Charlie Iwuege took me into his band.

In 1962, Charlie took me to Liberia where we played for President Taubman of Liberia.

When we returned to Lagos, we moved to Kano. Soon after the Nigerian crisis began, so I left for Eastern Nigeria.

One man, Kingsley Bassey, from Calabar took me. We moved to Onitsha, from there to Port Harcourt, then to Aba. From Aba we moved over to Calabar where another crisis occurred. So, I left finally to my home-town. I was in my home-town during the Nigerian crisis and war. When the crisis ended, I had no interest in going out again.

I played for soldiers during the war to entertain them. Both the Biafran and Nigerian soldiers asked me to entertain them, because Owerri was sometime under Nigeria, then under Biafra, and then under Nigeria. In all, I stay put in my home-town, Nekede. Whether Biafra, I entertained them; whether Nigeria I entertained them.

I had no real group to call my own. With my guitar I joined the group I see. At one time I tried to have my own group which entertained soldiers and other people.

I remember names like Celestine Okeke from Obosi as well as Oby (Raphael Anusieyi) from Nnobi whom I played with from place to place. Their own was "bar-band."

My first number of my own was "*Aman si ukwu bu egwu, mu ewere nkem nye Bongo.*" This was a

1971 hit. I was inspired to do this number because of the events in the society; it was all proverbs. After that came the one I did in my full native tongue, "*Umuekwenaru' go.*" Also, I talked in proverbs saying that it is not good for us to maltreat one another. "*Chukwu enyegh aka, onye genye anyi*" was another one in 1972. It was about the struggle for land after the war. Then I followdd with another one, "*Umu Nnem, unu jisie ike,*" an advice to the people.

In spite of all these hot-sellers, what have I got? They play my record always and pay me nothing. I have made the name but no money. My record is always on radio. But "*God dey, nothing pass-am.*" I am happy that people recognize what I have done to make this country a better place for all of us with my music. I thank God for that.

## Herbert Udemba

(An offspring of Israel Nwoba's ministrel-highlife rhythms)

"My music entertains, educates, and counsels."

Music is in our blood. I took the place of my brother, Israel Nwoba, to show that music is truly in our blood.

I was born in 1939; started school at Government School Owerri. I inherited musical talent from my father who is a singer. My mother and sisters were also singers. Singing was just in our family; they all are traditional music specialists. I grew up and was interested in music during my school days. There was one group which I was at the head. They are called children's group (*Otu Umuaka*) or the age grade, I was singing for them. After my primary education, I went to secondary school and still have that interest in music. In the church choir, I was one of the leaders in the Age Grade Traditional Group. After school, I decided that a white-collar job will not be my choice, so I said I will go into singing. I went into it to show the world that music is not a bad thing. It is quite good when you do it well.

I joined the N.A. (Native Authority) Police Band, Kano. We are the first to make it famous under the present Emir of Kano, Ado Bayero, when he was the superintendent of police. This was 1953 to 1955; I was then in the regular police force. We formed the N.A. Police Band with Emegeli Tola as our leader and trumpeter. I thought of leaving the Police Band to become a professional musician because musical talent is a hereditary one in our family; I did not want to be an "artificial musician." It was just in our blood, my brother, Israel Nwoba, who is now dead is an artist. I did one record titled "*Aya mma aya mma Israel Nwoba alaala.*" I have done sixteen records with Nigerphone (C.T. Onyekwelu) before his death. Then the war started and I left my instruments and went to war. Before I left for war, people from (Santa Isabel) Island of Fernando Po's Estelina Hotel came to Nigeria and took me with my group to Fernando Po, and kept us at the Esterlina Hotel as a station band under Oluvivo, the proprietor and the manager. I was at Calabar, at V.I.C. (Versatile Industrial Caterers Hotel), when they came and took me. I was playing there as a station band of the hotel; by then I had been very famous as a musician. Also, I was very popular because I speak seven languages.

I speak English, Spanish, French, Hausa, Yoruba, Efik, and Ijaw and the eighth is Igbo language being my mother-tongue. My band was called 'Herbert Udemba West African Babies Party.' I called it West African Babies Party because I am an African, but now I have changed it to 'Herbert Udemba and his Africali,' meaning Africa will live. I have started playing music before my brother, Israel, died. With that record, I wanted to tell the world that the person who died was my brother. I have replaced him to show that we are musicians by birth. The record I played says that Israel has died, and Herbert the brother has returned from "French" (Northern Camerouns was a French Protectorate) to take his place; that is I lived in Camerouns but came to Nigeria to do my recordings. My first wife is a Camerounian. I started playing professionally in 1979 but I started recording in 1958 when I produced my first record after the death of Israel. The record was titled "*Ema give me bottom belle cool my heart.*" I played this number because my wife is a foreigner while I am a Nigerian. She as a foreigner should tell me the truth to reassure me so that we can live in peace. The record sold greatly, almost every couple had it in Nigeria and abroad. It also made husbands and wives to live in harmony. I am happy that the record brought harmony to families.

All these languages I speak, I have lived in those places where they are spoken. I have lived in the French country for nine years. I lived in Gabon for three years, in Spain for two and half years. I worked under the Police Force in Kano; I've lived in Calabar; went to school in Rivers. I used to go to many places where musicians were performing at the Camerouns. I showed interest and sometimes asked them to play while I sang. They make comments such as: "this man, he will be a good musician." They asked me why I can't come out as a full musician and I'll tell them that the time has not yet come.

I worked at C.D.O (Camerouns Development Co-operation); I was once a nurse in the hospital; I was also a soccer-star; It was because of football that I was employed at the General Hospital, Tiko. It was in Tiko that I came out fully as a professional musician with the name "Herbert Udemba and His African Babies Band." That was in 1958 after my first record "*Bottom Belle.*" I did the one of Israel's death after I did "Zimiro's death," "*Bolingo,*" "*Ufodu na-aja anyi mma,*" *Udodu neto eto*" and "*Agam ekoroithe gogbue onwei.*" There was one I did to tell the people that I have stepped back to music (i.e. after my musical career has been disturbed by financial problems and I have lost my instruments in the war). I did "*Onye did nma na-azu?*" "*Ahamefula.*" I did "*Ahamefula*" because God has been so kind and has given me a wife and blessed me with children. Without children or a child, all your wealth, riches, millions and billions are nothing and your name is gone for ever. After listening to this music, many people went in search of the record. In "*Agam aghara uwa oso n'ihi ego,*" I said nobody should kill himself or herself because of material things. Nobody should kill a fellow human being, what I see today I'll take. I will follow my God because God is the one who has everything. It was to make people have faith and endurance, even though the person is suffering. Just like Job who suffered but because of his faith and endurance, was rewarded.

About Nzimiro, he was the Mayor of Port Harcourt in the days of Does; he was one who was loved by everybody; he was very humane and of good behaviour. So when he died, I decided to tell the world that such a person is no more. All these records have been waxed. I have more than sixty unreleased pieces.

Out of the unreleased pieces, one is saying "*wetue aka n'ihe ojo, ejila ehuhu amicha mkpuru aka n'ihi na i gaghi a fama ya n'elu.*" This was composed in June 1984 but has not been recorded. I was moved by what I saw in the last administration, how we were mis-administered, how we were later left at the background and how things turned round and we were very much deceived. Anyway, life is not straight. I never knew that these people will now be questionable characters. Therefore, people should not run faster than their age, to avoid untimely death. Slow and steady wins the race.

## Bongos Ikwue

Here is a musician who listened to his calling and dropped his pursuit in Electrical Engineering at the University in order to preach love, peace and brother-hood through "African country music:"

> What is 'failure' to the businessman is not failure to the artist ... the purpose of writing songs is to convey a message to the people...the commercial success of an album is dependent on a number of factors, most of them outside the control of the artist...music entrepreneurs and recording companies have a great hand in the so-called failure of any album.

You don't start being a musician unless you think that it a profession through which you can express those things that are in harmony with human specie or human ways... just as you don't start being a medical doctor without a desire to be kind in mankind.

I believe firmly that there is one truth and many lies... I believe in one God...You cannot pick up God in the street because you found Him with broken leg...The man with the broken leg must be your fellow man...You cannot go to bed with 'God's wife'...He is not like you.

I am looking forward to the day Moslems will go to church and Christians will go to the mosques and shake hands without worshipping one God in different ways...

I was born in 1942 in Otukpo, Benue State. I went to primary school for a few years in Otukpo. Then I went to Jos to complete my primary and school education. But I eventually completed it between Jos and Kaduna, in St. Luke's School, Jos (1953 to 1954); and from 1954 to 1955 in St. Michael's School, Kaduna. I came back to St. Luke's Jos, and finished up In 1956. I went to St. Paul's Secondary School, Zaria, finished between 1957 and 1961 and obtain my West African School Certificate (WASC). I went to Kano in 1963 for my Higher School Certificate Education. I got through that and gained admission to Ahmadu Bello University, Zaria.

I was influenced in my childhood by my late brother who was in the Police Force. I lived with him and had a whole lot of records to listen to. I was influenced by the fact that I lived in a house where many records were played; every evening and early in the morning, we listened to records.

At A.B.U. Zaria, as an Electrical Engineering student, I began discovering myself. I am one absolutely certain that human beings should not do things which they would regret afterwards. At every step in my life when I take a decision, I take a very positive one. The decision is influenced entirely by me. I always take a decision before announcing to my friends what 1 am about to do. When I wanted to do music, i.e to leave A.B.U., I told my friends after taking my decisions and right now I have no regrets, whatsoever. I am glad I went to the University and know what it actually looked like. I still have a lot of friends there: classmates who are lecturers, senior lecturers, doctors, professors, etc and we still interact in a very friendly atmosphere. I have travelled extensively; had different experiences and met all kinds of people.

I am also glad that I am still in touch with all my friends they come to the studio and catch up on old times.

Ella, a lunatic; calm and paradoxically saner than most other human beings, was a subject of a song dedicated to him. He played with all sorts of children. Every kid was made to laugh as a result of his activities. Ella "a mad man," succeeded in bringing life and colour to Otukpo town, otherwise it would have been dull. When you pass along the streets, you will see him performing funny events which arrested the attention of every kid; young and old. Everybody became happy in spite of the man's misfortunes.

I recall his life very vividly and played my music with the mood Ella's life created for the community. So, I dedicated a track, in one of my albums, to him. I used Ella's own language in the music (language formed out of that with which he played with kids). My song was a tribute to him.

Before I was known nationally, I was playing in Kaduna with some partners. I played in the University with a group called the "Unibello Brothers" which I led when I was still a student at Ahmadu Bello University (ABU). Most students knew me well and attended my shows at any cost. It was actually during my higher school education that I had my first song the "*Kubana Boys*" and the school recognized me. At St. Paul's Secondary School, the boys recognized me. I got all kinds of nicknames because I played and sang at "House Parties."

I had been growing slowly but surely with music all through my life. I just happened to be known in our country when my songs were released on discs. The album that really brought me into limelight and made the greatest sale was "Still Searching." Some people said that I had a break at a certain point because I produced an album which was a failure' I didn't have any break. Indeed, there was a publication which said "Bongos takes a break." 1 never took a break. I have never taken any break. About the album which they allegedly reported as a failure, I have this to say: the word "failure" or "success" is so relative to so any things in terms of money; in terms of quality of the record and in terms of acceptability by the listeners, it is not easy to define. As of now, a lot of people make demands for my albums continuously. As an artist, there is nothing like failure if the purpose is to write a song that conveys a message to the people. What is "failure" to the businessman is not failure to the artist. To a businessman failure means that a record hasn't sold too much. Probably, the recording company hasn't made enough effort to publicize the record, still the failure is credited to the artist's inability to express a message and carry it to the listeners.

As far as I am concerned my most successful album is the one called "Lagos" which had many songs that carried direction and purpose. Songs that talk about the undertone of religious differences that goes on all over the world, songs about pick-pockets and songs like "Man and Man" that talk about the Nigerian Civil war. To an artist, an album is a success if the message therein goes to the people, but to any other individual, it is a failure if the message did not reached him or her. So, I do not regard any of my albums as a failure and I am very happy to maintain that view.

Some said I was trying to be a rather strange Nigerian because I witnessed a decline in the quality of my work and I did not hang on just to make a name. I still wonder what they mean by "decline." In what sense was the word applicable? If one had a functional pause in order to understand ones self better, is that a decline? To me, one of the things in this world is that you must recognize yourself, know who you are. You don't just come out and be a star boxer without developing your strength and skills or without being a strong man. You don't start being a doctor without a desire to be kind to mankind. First of all, you must search yourself. You don't start being a musician unless you are gifted and you want to exploit your talent, not because you want to make cheap name, money or because you think it's a job that will suit you, or because you think it's God's gift. It has to be because you think there lies a profession through which you can express those things that are in harmony with human specie or the human ways. In my opinion, if "success" came at all, it just came as a bye-product of the main goal. The main thing is the decision to do what I think I can do and what I have the gift to do. Other things like popularity and wealth are bye-products of the main thing.

My first recording was in 1972; that first album was a rhumba rhythm called "You can't hurry the Sunrise." Others are "Sitting on The Beach," "Turn my Girl," "Thunder with Lagos," "Something Good," "Tear Drops," "Cock-crow at Dawn," etc. I cannot really talk about influences from my family as regards my talents in music. My parents were never singers. I heard that my father did a special dance when he was younger but he was not a singer. My wife too, couldn't have influenced me because I had started singing before we got married. Relations did not influence me but they all contributed in one way or the other, they gave me moral support and liked what I produced. They are happy because I am happy in my profession. Influence in my musical career has been mainly through my own "listening," it is a constant thing; it could be a tingling of a distant sound; it could be a particular sound you like. The sum total of all these interactions can evolve and come out with you writing a brand new song. So, every artist is influenced one way or the other, and that is how it is with past and present music; but the main thing is that the artist must learn or has to or strive to retain his or her own identity. The artist would never want to be like anybody else but like himself, because there are no two faces in the world that are exactly the same. I started as professional musician as far back as 1968 in Kaduna. The first professional group I had was called "Bongos Roof Toppers" in Kaduna because we played in the city and regarded ourselves as the "Toppest." When I moved to Lagos, I changed the name to "Groovies" and we have remained so to date. The members are constantly changing, one leaves for one reason or other and the process continues, in spite of the fact that on my own initiative, they do a group album from time to time; "Soul-Prayer" is one such album. Some presume that I am the one grooming my cousin to turn a professional. I am not grooming him, he is grooming himself.

I believe I am very talented; I write my songs; I have a cousin I admire as a person and he too admires me as a person. He is hardworking and talented so I have a lot of interest in him. I have never given him lectures in any form nor have I written any songs for him in any form, he just happens to be very gifted in his own right. I like the way he does his things, he has a chance of coming out sometime in the future, and I wish him good luck. He has my moral support.

I have very nice and cordial relationship with other Nigerian musicians. I stay very busy currently on one thing or the other; I have not much time left for socialization. What made me do the album called "Songs 1 like to Sing" is my admiration for the works of other artists. There are five songs on the LP, only one was written by me; others were rearranged by me. The artists are the late Sam Cook, Tom Davis, Kenny Rogers and Brook Benton. I rearranged and sang them.

Neither Kenny Rogers nor any of the rest knows me, but an artist never ever could know all those who know him. I don't accept that these artists affected my style. Nobody can really affect anybody's style unless one deliberately wants his style affected. Style is a gift; the quality of my voice, the way I talk, my choice, my parents, the size of my lips, the total genetics of my being, all of these influence me as an individual and they are bound to influence my style.

But when you consciously and deliberately want to change your God-given style, because you want somebody's style, then you become a phoney. So, nobody has affected my style; my style is mine, what made me Bongos is my style.

As I said earlier on, influences do come as a result of "listening." Somehow, Sam Cooke, Celestine Ukwu, Joe Nez, etc can be heard through me. The ways they lay emphasis on words or on instruments like guitar and flute sink into my subconscious somewhere. All of these could be said to affect the sum total of my work but they cannot change my identity. So, I have retained my identity.

I preach the gospel of living together, like I did in the track of a man called Christopher, because, in spite of religious differences, he is the same person as Mustafa. I believe firmly that there is "One Truth" and "Many Lies." There is only one truth about any event and there are many versions of it that are only lies. So, having said that clearly, I believe that there has to be one God, it doesn't matter how you conceive Him. Whatever religion, whatever form you conceive Him, He is God and people, through the years, have worshipped God in various forms. If you truly worship and respect the Almighty God, then you respect all forms of human beings because there is a relationship between God and man. No one can really, ever do any good to God. You cannot pick God up in the street because you found him with broken leg and you charitably decide to take Him to the hospital. The man with the broken leg must be your fellow man. You cannot go to bed with God's wife; He is not like you, you cannot steal from God directly but you can do all these things to your fellow man. You can stab another fellow man; you can lie against a fellow man and put him in prison. So, relationship in religion directly lies between God who has a very indirect relationship with man. You cannot not preach about God, talk about God unless you are able to live with your fellow man in complete and perfect harmony because therein lies the relationship I am talking about.

## Dr. Sir Warrior
*The Oriental Brothers Igbo-Idiom lyricist, interpreter, and spiritualist.*

It is good for people to understand first what the singer is saying. It's just like going to Church with your Bible to preach to the congregation.

Through music you can preach the gospel. And people like listening to gospels more when they are musically preached.

Things may go well for you in this world while in the next you may find yourself in big trouble.

Respect is lacking. It is one of the factors that help in nation building.

Born in Mbaise Local Government Area in the year August 28 1947, I attended primary and secondary schools in that area. I was very much interested in music as a child. I used to go to any ballroom dance organized anywhere around me. I was the sole leader of many cultural music groups in my village. People come to hire me on any cultural occasion to entertain them. As time went on, I joined the "Andyman International Band," led by John Ikediani. that was in 1970. All my songs, nobody taught me how to sing them; it's a gift from God. All the time in my songs, I preach how men can live their lives without regrets. It's just like gospel songs; I seldom sing songs that are not gospel-like in nature. I do not sing for anybody's sake or because of somebody. All I sing is for everybody, whoever hears what I say can surely grab one useful thing out of it.

In Ikediani's group in 1970, we did only an album with the title "*Oke no n'olulu o nwere nso?*" Things didn't always go well; we were not in good terms, I mean John Ikediani and the rest of us. We seldom see him, he moves his own way so we decided to stay on our own and went to a man who owned a hotel in Ikeja. That was in 1973; the man gave us his own band and eventually some Camerounians came and joined us. Those in the group by then were Dan Satch, Kabaka, Ichika, Awila and me.

The hotel owner asked us to come and play in the East (at home) in December, 1973. We did so and went back to Lagos in 1974. In February 1974, we produced our own record titled "*The Chi nyere m Onye ananam*" (Nobody should take what God gave me). By then we were with Decca (West Africa); Decca gave us instruments and we played by ourselves, until 1978 when Kabaka left us and formed his own band called "Kabaka International Band." We had no trouble but we all felt that we were all stars and the company itself is making a lot of money by then. We said since Kabaka is determined to break off, we can't beg him or try to make him not to go that it's okay by us.

The group was then left with Ichika, Akwila Dan Satch and me. We went on till 1979 when, Ichika, and Awila went off and formed their own band called "Great Orientals."

It remained only Dan Satch and me; we played together up to 1980. Dan Satch formed his own band and I, warrior did likewise. My band is called "Sir Warrior and his Oriental International Band."

In our first record (i.e. the Original Oriental Group) "The *Chi nyere m Onye ananam,*" we were trying to say that whatever God gave a man, nobody should go snatch or take it away from the man. Whatever God gave you is yours, the same thing with me; it is not achieved through jealousy, greed or killing. Anything God says you'll be, you'll certainly turn out to be that thing.

I can say that the record made great sales; yes, it sold very much. It was the one that popularized us. Up till today I am the vocalist in all the songs. I did the vocals in the whole records.

All records produced by the group were taken as the group's favourite; they all got gold disc for the group. Even the company recording them made excellent sales with them. In all my records, there's not one I can select as the best. I meditate a lot before singing and I strive to make the present one better than the last one. After recording they all attain the same level of quality. It's only the public that can say which one they like most.

I made one record called "*Chi awu ofu*" -a worker or sufferer must get his pay. It is one of those philosophical saying that he who works must eat what he earns or what he worked for. I made "The *Oma*" with the group in 1974 after the first one, then "*Jide nke gi kam jide nkem,*" that was my own record in 1980 when I and Dan Satch separated. I made it after doing "*Ana eri aku, a na-bia*" also in 1980.

There is "*Mmadu Mezie ndu ya, O keta oke n'aka Chineke*" in 1983. It is only God who rewards all men; man cannot get his reward from fellow man. Then there is "*Uwan kea sef,*" anything we have in this world belongs to God. There are people who have money, but they want to get more and more of it, forgetting that there are some who have none, who suffer and die of hunger and thirst. All these are sentimental songs. They touch human feelings. "*Ima onyebu onye*" was made by Dan Satch and me in 1978. Anybody you see, you know he or she is a human being like you but what or who he or she is you cannot tell. It is only God that knows who is who.

People should be humane and considerate. We don't know one another; we only see one another as human beings created by God. What one is thinking is not what the other is thinking.

One thing about my music which is why people love it so much is that it is always like an advice. It is not all records that are easy to understand. It is good for people to understand first what the singer is saying. It's just like going to church with your Bible to preach to the congregation.

Through music you can preach the gospel and people like listening to gospels more when they are musically preached.

As a well-known country in the universe, Nigeria has the problem of poor understanding. In other words, people have one thing and instead of sticking to that, they cast eyes on other things which are mostly not within their reach. Respect is also lacking;

it is one of the factors that help in nation building. Obey the government, do what you are told which you believe to be the right thing. There's no gain in disobedience. Have you considered that those who are now rich suffered to be rich before they could get it? And now that they have got it, they forget those under them, probably those who helped them to be rich.

It is always the case that when a person is suffering and eventually comes out, he or she feels that everything is O.K. for him/her. But it is not like that; you may be feeling O.K. today and tomorrow it changes. Things may go well for you in this world, while in the next you may find yourself in big trouble.

I have a strong belief that whatever I do for the betterment of myself or to my fellow man, it is God's will that I should do it. If not, that thing will not succeed.

I sing native tunes. Now, in this country, Nigeria, our young musicians prefer or have special likeness for rock, pop, anything that is disco and which the Whites play. I know that in our traditional music, we have as much materials as those abroad.

You can see that those who make foreign music do not get what they want in music. People like Sonny Okosun are more progressive in their music because he combines his native language with the Whiteman's. He doesn't altogether fill his records with foreign words. The whites are not ready to buy our record; they might be interested but they would like to get it free.

Even our grand papas and mamas at home, they do not like these foreign records or local ones with foreign language. They don't understand it a single bit. What they know is those ones they understand.

And if the government should do something, it will be banning foreign records and artists in the country. Also, the T.V. and Radio stations should stick strictly in featuring our native artists and their products. Abroad, they do not feature Nigerian artists unless he or she spends a huge amount of money to have him/her featured for only a few minutes. It is obvious that I am not happy with the way Nigerian artists (especially those in traditional music) are treated.

It is most shameful that when these artists play their foreign music, their people don't seem to know that it is their brothers who are playing, because they sound too foreign to be appreciated. Nigerian foreign-based musicians are not popular; whatever they do, let them bear in mind that they are from somewhere, let them not forget their mother and father-tongues.

I am the Vice-Chairman (Imo State) of PMAN. The organization is making a lot of effort in stopping piracy in the country. It has minimized the growing use of cassettes which makes musicians not to be what they should be i.e. not succeeding financially. The recording companies are the only people that are entitled to cassette productions and at times, most of these cassettes spoil the image of the artist. When the government stops this "cassetting," artists would at least be able to have a say in their own products.

My real name is Ezewuiro Chris Obinna. People nicknamed me WARRIOR. I did not choose it by myself. 1 am also a good footballer; my adventure as a child was music. I play to entertain my people. All my neighbours in the village cannot forget how I used to sing and play to them on any occasion.

I belong to an age grade. I am married and have three boys and a girl. There is nothing that 1 have which gives me as much happiness as my music. Also, 1 can't think of owning anything except musical talents. I am not going to do any other thing except music till I die. I am alright with what I have achieved; I have an offspring to take after me like I took after my parents.

When I was following Rex Lawson's band about as a very young fan of his, I knew in my heart that music is what my God had given me and that one day I will fulfil that talent. I knew within me that it is what I will do. So, I followed those who were doing it. Now I know, and I am quite sure that I have attained their level. Most of my songs were well-known tunes which were sung in my village during special occasions. The only difference is that I use mainly modem instruments to go-in-tune with the modem musical world.

I used to listen to the elderly men in my area and was able to catch many proverbs from them. I also use the proverbs which come from my own knowledge of life.

For instance: "*Nwanyi okpinwa na-acho ka o gbue nwe o bughi ya muru ma Chukwu ekweghi ya*" --that is, "a childless woman or mother is always unhappy when she sees a face of a child; she doesn't love children; another one "*Anyi loro uwa nime abali, anyi amaghi ebe chi si wee fod*" -meaning - "when a child is born, he or she doesn't know where he/she was born; doesn't know who gave birth to him/her. Then by the grace of God the child will start living a normal life, not knowing when to excrete or urinate. After some years the child will be able to have control over some of these natural occurrences.

The proverbs I use in my songs are so many, so numerous that it is not easy to list them unless there was enough time.

Since God gave me musical talent which I set out to exploit, I haven't been in any "skin-pain" or misfortunes. My music life has been smooth and steady; I am not sure of the future, but for the past years there hasn't been any "*palaver,*" well, some call me a superstar. The package I will release in the near future cannot be discussed until they come out, and people will know what it looks like or what it will be. It is like saying that the taste of the pudding is in the eating. After the food has been cooked, the only way to know what it tastes like is by eating it. The taste of a record is determined only when the record has been released and played.

I really have many records for the future. You will be hearing my voice continuously on records. Even if I am old, I'll still be playing music. I still have words of advice for the society in future.

## Ferdinand Ohams

TV and Radio houses' "come today, come tomorrow" attitude towards the payment of artists' fees is really bad.

Radio houses use artists' works to prepare jingles for commercial companies, yet in spite of the fees they collect from such companies, nothing accrues to the artist.

I compiled 'Love *Nwantinti* which I called 'Eline Series'... Onitsha people's moon-lit folksong.

I am the leader and founder of the "Sensational Comrades Rock Band" based in Enugu. I am a pop star. I was born at Uba Umuaka in Nkwere-Isu Local Government Area of Imo State; southern part of Nigeria on the 4$^{th}$ of May, 1950.

I attended St. Mary's Primary School, Umuaka, where I started music with the school's brass band. I also attended St. Saviour's Secondary School, Umuaka. Later I did Salesmanship in the National School of Salesmanship in England. I like traditional music just like my father and mother; they were good singers of traditional music during their own days.

So, I inherited music making from them and I have played with groups like "Green Vergineers" led by Gentleman Mike Ejeagha. That was after the Nigerian Civil War (otherwise called Biafran War). A drummer, singer, and what have you, that's me. As a competent musician, I left "Green Vergineers and joined a pop group called "the Wavelengths" with some of my good friends led by Peter Ighile, a Nigerian Air Force Officer. From "the Wavelengths," I joined another gentleman's band, "Celestine Ukwu and his Philosophers Band" in October, 1971 and played with him until October 1976. I switched over to "Hotel Presidential Trio" led by Uncle Mike Obianwu.

He contributed a lot in the making of the folk-singer, Nelly Uchendu. I compiled "Love *Nwantinti*," which I called 'Elina Series' with the help of Uncle Mike Obianwu and Justline Akuata, the "bassist" of the Trio. "Elina Series," which is called "Love *Nwantinti*' today was drawn from Onitsha peoples' moonlit folksongs. "Love *Nwantinti*' is the best and hottest number of the "Hotel Presidential Trio," that was long before it was recorded on commercial discs.

"Love *Nwantinti*' was usually played at the Hotel Presidential Garden by special request. Some Europeans who enjoyed the way I shouted "*Ewo-Ewo-Ewo*' each time the number was played showed their appreciations for Igbo cultural tunes. Nigerians also joined in the craze for "Love *Nwantinti.*"

As an ambitious musician, I left the "Trio" and formed my own musical group called "The Comrades Rock Band" with the help of some of my friends. After the birth of the group, I wrote a song I called "*Igba-aka-bia-I lum*' which means "do you want to marry me without cash." But unfortunately, another group called "Sweet Breeze" recorded it before me. Their second album became a hit because of that track.

Right now, "The Comrades Rock Band" has two albums in the market; "Mr. Love" and "Hosty World." We also have "unpublished" albums which are not to be recorded with the "*Monkey dey work, Baboon dey Chop*' type of recording companies. All we want is "*you chop, I chop.*" The attitude towards musicians is bad; they cheat musicians and even discourage them from ever wanting to be musicians by not paying them their royalties fully, thereby denying them artistes' entitlements. I am even really bitter over that issue. Some companies bootleg and pirate musicians' works, which is one of the main reasons why the Performing Musicians Association of Nigeria was formed.

T.V. and Radio houses' "come today, come tomorrow" attitude towards the payment of artists' fees is also really bad. At times when these Broadcasting Stations fail to get good artists for their programmes because of their poor treatment of the artists, they go in for cheap artists for their cheap programmes. Radio houses use artists for their cheap programmes, radio houses use artists' works to prepare jingles for commercial companies and in spite of the fees they collect from such companies, nothing accrues to the artists.

I can claim that I am industrious. I have made some musical research and have come out with certain facts. If you listen carefully to all the successful records made by the Blacks, the world over, which we appreciate and buy here today, you will find out that 90% of them have our traditional feelings and only a bit of Western touch to blend. So, for any pop musician in this part of the world to record music, he or she expects to market commercially, the musician must use a kind of traditional background and combine both traditional and Western "feelings." I can also claim that I am a "music superstar" and "king maker" because I contributed and helped so much in making artists like Jide Obi, Nelly Uchendu, William Onyeabo, Biddy Uchendu and others. In fact, I did very much during the productions of Celestine Ukwu's albums and Professor Sonny Oti's albums, respectively, as far as musical backing is concerned. In the case of Sonny Oti, I mean his album "*Nigeria Go Survive."* I am really a figure in the Nigerian music scene. My hobby ranges from swimming, foot-balling, dancing to film acting.

# Nellie Uchendu
*An Igbo folk-song singing superstar*

> We musicians have tried all along to help the government in nation building... We have done quite a lot.

> ... I went home happy for helping to 'restore' the life of a dying Catholic priest with my songs

> Vocalists come out much stronger than instrumentalists in African Music...By this I mean that the Voice says it all...

I was born in a family where almost all the members were good singers, i.e talented in music. My dad was a clergyman in the Anglican Church (a Catechist). I took part in the school choir, church choir, etc. When I grew up, I found out that my father was very interested in music, so was my mother. She has a beautiful voice even better than mine; my mother had always dominated the singing group during church choir activities, the harvest day activities and the harvest day thanksgiving occasions. She directs and organizes the women.

A talented person is identified from his or her childhood behaviour. If one is talented, the person starts at an early age, to show his or her arts work or craft. Talents are generally displayed from childhood; there is no way for one to hide one's talent, like me. The way I started, nobody told me to join the choir. It is just that during choral singing, one can always find me trying to belong, my father, being the parish priest. There was a particular occasion when they were having their usual choir practices, I came to the church and crept in to join them because I was virtually interested. They were learning a very nice song and I was singing it without being aware that my voice was coming out so loud that the choirmaster enquired about the voice, and they pointed at me.

That song was difficult for them to learn but I sang it accurately. So, the choir-master asked me to come and direct the voices on the treble side. I came out and sang. My father, who was looking for me, saw me singing in the church. He was then very mad with me but the master begged that my father should allow me to continue singing because my voice was so nice and I dominated the whole group. But my father would not listen, he insisted that I should come out and help my mother in the kitchen. From then I started sneaking out without their knowledge to participate in the choir practices. As time went on, I started wearing the choral robe and took part in the choral singing during service.

Within a short time, I started being popular with my voice. During my classes one to three in

Ogidi Girls Secondary School, I used to organize cultural singing group every Friday or at times, once monthly. Interested students went to the prefects in charge to write down their names. I was then fond of singing. I used to sing songs like "*Malaika*" etc. Every Friday, I used to sing during Social Nights and it got to the extent that my principal seemed to notice when I was absent. The principal used to ask about me if I didn't appear.

I started being really popular from then and there. I also took part in drama productions. In my Form two or three, I was the leading actress in a play we presented in the school entitled 'The Millionaires.' I was the Millionaire. I wore my principal's dress which was fantastic, superbly made, a sort of costume for drama. Apart from that, the principal herself dressed me and it was really something to reckon with. In my Form three, auditioning of voices took place in the school and I didn't join them. I was in the hostel and did not want to do it to give the rest of the girls a chance. I was appointed to do the audition of voices. The reason for not coming out was that some girls had started being jealous of me, and I did not want to break that basket of jealousy.

Because of my good voice, I was befriended by a mistress who started to invite me to her house. In school, I wasn't only popular with my singing and acting, I was known also for hair-plaiting (the best hair-plaiter in the whole school). Whenever I want to plait a girl's hair, the girl would start announcing to the whole school that I had come to do her heir. The thing got to a stage that I even plaited my principal's hair and those of other mistresses; I was naturally gifted. I was also good in domestic activities like cooking, sewing or designing dresses. I designed the costume which I wore when I represented Nigeria in some Musical Festivals. At the Eastern Nigeria Festival of Arts in 1964 and 1968, I featured in eight events and I bagged eight good certificates, given to me in the presence of the whole school.

My music master then was the popular Mr. Sam Ojukwu, the pioneer of the whole thing. He taught me all the music I sang. During the Nigerian Civil

War, I was sent on a course to Abak (Cross River), a School of Agric, to do a course on Agriculture. During the end of the course, a kind of social evening was organized where they had some activities like singing, drama, etc and I featured in the singing. The Rev. Fathers and Rev. Sisters, who were the Governing Council of the Holy Family and Holy Child Colleges, as well as of the Hospitals, were invited to come and watch our social evenings.

After the occasion, a Rev. Father congratulated me and told me that they were thrilled by my performances, and my beautiful voice. He also said that I should not leave my voice untrained. They were particularly interested and would like to do what they could for me to get the training. Other Rev. Fathers, who are held in high esteem in the society, recognized me as gifted in entertaining shows.

One day, I was very sick and the Rev. Sisters came to swim at the Agric training premises. Somebody asked me to go and tell them that I was ill and may be they would help take me to a hospital. My friend went and told the Sisters, who came running to where I was and within some seconds, they were people around me praying. After the prayers, the Sisters said I should follow them and I did so. I sat in front of a 504 saloon car, driven by Sis. Dr. McSweeney (She is now dead, may her soul rest in peace). They took me to their hospital and did everything possible to make sure I became well again. They were always praying and there was even a time I got so bored with their continuous prayer. After all kinds of treatments, I was sent back to our base. From then, I became friendly with them all. When I was about to leave the institution, they organized a kind of cultural display to entertain the wounded soldiers from the war-front at the Holy Child College's hall. I was asked to come and entertain them with my group called the "Hill Top Singers." I was also allowed to take the group to Holy Child to entertain the wounded soldiers.

That evening, we sang before a packed auditorium full of Rev. Fathers, and Sisters. The wounded soldiers were about fifty or so. But the rest were Rev. Fathers and Sisters. I had never seen such a number of missionaries like that in my life. Had it been I had not been very high-spirited because of the way they called upon me to sing, I wouldn't have been able to stand the huge audience. I sang songs that I learnt during my days at primary and secondary schools.

There was another occasion when I was invited by a Rev. Sr. Dr. who was working at T.T.C to entertain the students there. I went and that was the occasion I had to try "to raise a dying priest with my songs." The hall was again packed full of Rev. Fathers, Sisters, and students. I did not even know what I was singing except that they were beautiful songs; at that time I was still under eighteen. I went home with presents and was happy for "helping to restore" the life of a dying Catholic priest with my songs. The truth is that the Priests and the Rev. Sisters knew that my songs could cheer up the sick Priest. In fact, after a few songs in English, half-way through my presentation, the Priest started talking. I stopped singing and he beckoned me to come closer. I did and he held my hand, touched me and felt the whole of my hands as one blind. He said "The Voice is like Mahille Jackson's but the skin is African skin. How can such an 'African skin' sing like Mahllle Jackson or Dustus Springfield rather?" It was a big improvement for him to be able to talk. The Sister thanked me saying "Our Rev. Father is now able to talk. Can't you see that you have a powerful voice that can raise the dying or the dead?" At a certain time, I went to Okigwe on posting during the War. I was working with the Food Production Directorate. At Okigwe, even when I was in the office, I kept singing, I disturbed people with my songs. For instance, there was a lady friend of mine who now works in the Internal Revenue (Enugu). The last time she saw me, she said "Do you remember those days when you used to disturb me with your songs. If Nigeria were a wealthy country, people like you would have by now become millionaires but I guess you are now in money." I told her I was not in money yet, that the money is not coming but the name which I set out to make is coming.

There was a secretary by name Ben Okagbue. He used to be the Commissioner of Boys Scout, at Okigwe. He had some sons and daughters studying overseas. One of his sons knew how to play the violin and one of his daughters was a good singer. Because of the talents in his family, I used to visit them frequently. Whenever I went there, I would ask his son to play the violin for me. Mr. Okagbue once overheard me singing to his son's violin and suggested that they should organize a little band, so that they could go and entertain the Biafran Armed Forces in military hospitals. Mr. Okagbue was able to make an addition to the orchestra and launched it. We started going out to entertain the wounded soldiers. We sang classical music, pop, rock, anything that came our way. That was when I started learning how to sing pop songs. And as it is, children who are trained abroad basically like pop music; Mr. Okagbue's children were interested in pop, but I was interested in highlife.

So, we combined the two; Mr. Okagbue named the group "The Spangle." After the war, the East Central State organized a festival to raise funds. I featured in the activities and got two certificates in two events. I belong to one or two choral groups in Anambra State Musical Society. There was a time I even joined the Federal Radio Corporation choral group at Enugu. But I was still restless and dissatisfied.

A group at Enugu Hotel Presidential led by Mike Obianwu became a regular rehearsal and operational base for me. Right from childhood, I was fond of following musicians about to wherever; I did so with Celestine Ukwu and Harry Mosco. So I had to formally apply to join Mike Obianwu and his group. Mike accepted and the formality was completed by the Hotel Presidential manager who offered me the contract. Soon after, many people began to admire the group, people started enjoying our production and new fans started flowing in as my popularity in Enugu grew.

I came home and saw a letter inviting me to

perform during the prestigious Festac '77 at Lagos. What an honour for me to perform at the Second All Black Festival of Arts and Culture at that global level. I couldn't believe it. I was thus privileged to be a member of the Festac Choir and a Nigerian highlife band led by Zeal Onyia. The Festac Choir was led by Prof. Laz Ekwueme; I was one of the soloists to do the Kenyan song. I made a demo of an Igbo folk song "Love *Nwantiti*" before the Festac so I took it to Lagos. I thought Zeal Onyia was going to work on that particular number; he gave me that impression, but he did not fulfil my dreams. Thus, after Festac, I summoned all the courage I could muster to release the album.

The background to the release of the album is memorable to me, ironically, because although the album hit top of the chart, the financial success did not come to me because of the kind of "verbal contract" I had with the Producer, Homzy Continental Enterprises. But my pleasure was that Homzy launched me to the disc world and that Mike Obianwu and my fans were inspirational sources. I owe the T. V a lot for exposing me; of course, it enriched their programmes and its quality, also the Radio at Enugu. I was thus inspired to release the second one titled "*Aka bu Eze*." After that, I followed up with Sonny Oti's song in his album "Late Nite Husband," which has remained a "chart buster." Sonny had invited me to sing the lead in that track which was also the title of his album because it was a satire against "*Waka-about-husbands.*"

Other numbers came to swell my repertoir: "Hossana," "Green Eagles," "Mama *Awusa*" and "*Ogadili gi mma.*" I had made about seven records (many fans always thought that "Late-Nite Husband" was my own composition - so they credit it to me in error). I had another one about "Papa and Mama" done with the mixed grill.

If a person does not have a musical voice talent, even if he drinks "*Ogbono* soup" three times a day, he will remain a person with no singing qualities. Even with a voice talent, "over-use by talking or crying could spoil the voice" according to some people. Some people also say that when they sing more than three songs, their song declines but 1 could sing even up to eight songs and my voice will continue to get clearer. The more I sing, the better my voice becomes. I don't drink anything like eggs which, according to some people, improve the voice. It has never been necessary for me to need supporting throat-lubricants.

So, I can say that I have a special gift - a beautiful voice -from God. My kind of voice is usually referred to as "*agbala* voice" (voice of the gods). Before any festival was performed in our village, the people would start to look for a female that has "*Agbala* voice," the voice that can project messages. Thus, my voice comes out more beautiful when I sing cultural songs. I can do songs in alien culture, like English, with professional ease, but not with traditional ease as when I take on our cultural songs. Thus, I am deeply-rooted in our culture and the excellence of it. That's why I am solid when I do Igbo folk songs.

Now, about the split in the Oriental group, vocalists usually come out stronger than instrumentalists in African music, no matter the experience or the artistry of the instrumentalists. By this, I mean that the voice says it all; nevertheless, the two cannot do without each other. But the person who holds the voice has the stronger instrument and in fact, in every-day life, the vocalists are paid more because no matter how you manipulate the instrument and nothing sweet is said at the background, though it will make sense, there will be no embellishment.

The vocalists are in a position to convey messages. When the first Executive President of Nigeria was about to be installed, in his message, he said that now musicians should strive towards nation building instead of singing "free" songs (lyrics without messages) or praising people, etc., that they should concentrate more on building up the nation. He said that some of them (musicians) can say something that can even change the minds of politicians like the latest Sonny Okosun's album - "Which Way Nigeria?"

It has done a lot to change the minds of the people. Musicians like the Juju music groups of Sunny Ade, Ebenezer Obey, the Waka Queen etc., all sing philosophical songs. I myself did one too when 1 sang "*Okwu di nlo.*" Right now in our country, people do not know how to relate to one another, particularly if money is involved. Even if one is the creditor and the other is the debtor, there are ways of settling the matter because "soft words soften the heart." Even in our every day life, if a wife wants to get something from her husband, all she needs is soft words; but when she goes all thunder and nagging, she will find it hard to get what she wants. Even if she gets it, it is not given whole-heartedly by her husband. Likewise in the office, if you want to show a junior colleague that you are the boss, then he will tell you that without him you can't do your job.

Musicians have tried to help the government in nation building all along. This time, let the government come and help us; musicians have done quite a lot. There was a review in the *Daily Star* by Denise Mbadugha. He said that there are difficulties encountered by musicians, especially female musicians. Actually, he said that a female musician in Nigeria may not find things easy.

In the olden days, there was a taboo against females participating in showbiz. People regarded her as a vain person, very irresponsible. But with the coming of female musicians like Miriam Makeba, Mary Afi Usua and others, our women started developing interest and the urge to exploit their musical talents.

My dreams in musical career are fulfilled with the prestigious award of National Honours conferred on me by the civilian Head of State. For my country to pick me out as a distinguished artist is not something to joke about. About a few weeks ago, the Federal Government sent me out to represent Nigeria in the Commonwealth Festival of Arts in London; the international "Who is Who in Music" has recognized me. It's certainly something to be proud of. Again, not many weeks ago, an indigenous airline has told me of their willingness to send me to London again. One recording company is about to send me abroad with

Sir Dr. Warrior.

I have not experienced a setback in my musical career, although I cannot say I feel at ease at the office where I work. I have learnt to accept whatever I'm offered there. Not even many people are aware that I work for the cultural division of the Ministry of Information. One would expect to hear a lot about me through my department. In foreign countries, for a star like me to be in that place, it will be headline on T. V and the dailies. Many people have told me to resign but I won't. The way I was brought up makes it impossible for me to act that way. I am aware that the government needs me.

I don't want to be an inconvenience to the people. I hope that in the near future, things will be better. Of course, queer things do happen in a musical career to give one second thought. Like when I was recording for a certain company; while in the studio, someone deliberately turn-off all the lights and I couldn't find the engineers working with me; I even stepped on a chair while trying to find my way. I believe it's got to do with tribal politics in Nigeria and things would have been worse if I were not careful. The following morning, the news would have been that I was murdered in cold blood in a studio.

It's not all that comfortable to combine a job in Civil Service with a musical career. Musical establishments and groups could employ me fully, but they have not done that. For now, they keep me very busy, which is satisfying.

I have always wished that there will be a time when there will be a Musical Group to be named the "Uchendus" because right now in my family almost everybody sings. My immediate younger sibling has released two albums "*Onye bu Nwanne m*" and "*Ka anyi kele Chineke.*" Another sister of mine is doing very well. She is also doing mass communication. The son in our family is also a singer. I keep hoping there will be a time when we will all have a kind of band (a family band). It's either a family band based on gospel songs or otherwise. I have hopes that by God's grace, these hopes will come to reality.

## Etubom Rex Williams

His father was one of the founders of the Salvation Army Church in his area. So, he learnt how to play the trumpet rather early.

> Be contented with what you have; beware of riches overnight; If you have nothing doing, better find something good to do. Half-bread is better than none ... Half-bread is better than going to steal and it's better than sitting idle.
>
> Think of the last day -the Lord's Day of Judgement. Seek after God now; throw away your juju, it won't save you.
>
> On that last day, there will be plenty of palm-wine but no time to drink; there will be food and none will have appetite and time for it; husband and wife will be torn apart from their love nest in the midst of chaos and confusion during accountability before God.
>
> This country needs the services of musicians to improve the moral standards of its citizens so that the future will be brighter for all of us through the fear of God and the love of God and one another.
>
> My father married eleven wives, with thirty-four children: seven boys and twenty-seven girls. I am the sixth boy. I am married; I have five children: three boys and two girls. My wife and children are still with me.
>
> I started music while in school in 1952. After standard six, I went in for a one year course at the Teacher Training College. My father was among the founders of Salvation Army Church in my area. Salvation Army had many musical instruments with which 1 used to learn. I am really talented as a musician. After school, I started playing the trumpet.
>
> I was inspired by one of my older brothers; he was then a band master of the Salvation Army Church. He now works for the Chronic Mental Department. I had the opportunity to learn the trumpet. I left for Enugu where I was employed in the Service Station of Transmitting Station doing a sort of

telecommunication

One day, I heard that E.T. Mensah of Ghana was coming to town. I was highly impressed by the way he sang, the way he put up his music. He projects the image and cultural heritage of his country. Mensah sang in Ghananian languages and that impressed me and he was also playing the trumpet which was my special instrument; I was really inspired.

When Mensah left, I decided to quit the Civil Service and move on to Lagos for a musical adventure. My father was very much against the idea, and thought of disowning me. He did not like me to become a musician while he was a teacher. While my father was still quarrelling over my determination to become a musician, one of my brothers came home from the United States of America. The family had some discussion about my ambition; my brother, Dr. James Esema, supported that I should be allowed to do what I like, because he himself had seen such professionals in the U.S.

My father then succumbed to my brother's argument and finally gave me some money to go to Lagos. In Lagos, I heard a lot about a band in Empire Hotel. I heard them playing some tune in the hall of the hotel. I went down to watch them and was surprised to see some Igbo men who were my friends. I asked them if I could play the trumpet. They granted my request. Everybody in the hall rose to dance to my trumpet display. I was very happy about the impression I made. 1 knew then that I could be a star with my trumpet. I went home with 300 (Three hundred pounds) cash from my successful display of the trumpet.

The following morning, Chief Kanu knocked on my door after introducing himself as the proprietor of the hotel; he offered me the post of a band-leader. I replied that I couldn't make up my mind then, but the man insisted. Then I asked for a few days to think about the issue but after two days somebody came from Welfarers Hotel; that person was a relation of mine by name Johnson. He told me that there was one madam who seriously wanted to see me at the hotel. I went with my relation to meet the madam (the owner of the Welfarers Hotel). There, I saw one Chief Ajayi and soon I started playing at the hotel.

People began to hear about "Rex Williams" and his music. This happened in 1960. As I was playing one day, Victor Olaiya came and offered me the post of a leader of his band which he said was playing at that same hotel. He managed to convince me and made sure I got a well-equipped and furnished house with good pay. My dance-band gained popularity. Victor Uwaifo was then my guitarist. The band was called to play during the visit of a well-known Professor Leo Sack and that was in 1961; 1 represented Lagos and played the trumpet very well. Victor Olaiya was there and was very much impressed by my performance. He talked to me after the show. By now many people knew me and were always eager to see me play the trumpet.

In 1966, during the crisis which followed the military coup, the band members ran away for their dear lives. I too escaped and at home I was given a warm welcome by my parents, because while I was away, I made a record which was very nice and which impressed my father.

I was invited by the then East Central State Government to perform in an occasion. I made a record which the Head of State, General Gowon, used to open an important occasion. He was so impressed that he granted me some loan to expand my work. It was from then that I was able to stand on my own.

My music was a sort of advice to the nation. Music can change people; if you give a message which says that stealing is not good, people will improve their moral standards because of the song and its meaning. They will fight against stealing for they have heard that it is not good.

I have made quite a number of other achievements since then but the most important is that this country needs the services of musicians to improve the moral standards of its citizens so that the future will be brighter for all of us through the fear of God and the love of God and one another.

## Prince Nico Mbarga
*The original composer of the popular top-of-the-chart 'Sweet Mother"*

During an interview with the British Broadcasting Corporation in London, the interviewer asked me if I can also play Western music, I asked him to mention any Whiteman who would play African music.

All these disco-pop music hardly have any message for our country; always talking about love: I love you, you love me, my baby, my this, my that...so much nonsense...no message worth listening to...and they are not known abroad.

Go to London, France and other European countries, you will see that 99% of artists on their screen are their own artists. But here in Nigeria, we have 95% foreign artists on our screens. We say we want to Nigerianize everything, but at the same time, we are taking foreign culture. You will be surprised that in the near future, some 2,000 years in the future, children who will be born then will not really know what *Oji* (kolanut) means because the traditions of the society shall have been wiped out.

Born in Abakaliki in the year 1950, 9 of April, my father, a Camerounian, had lived at Calabar. He left Calabar in 1922 and stayed at Abakaliki and married a Nigerian, who of course, is my mother. I started music in primary school. I used to play the xylophone. I came from a family that loved playing the xylophone.

My father taught me how to play the instrument. I used to play old songs like those of Rex Jim Lawson's with my xylophone.

One day, around 1961, when I was in standard three, I was playing and my headmaster, Mr. Chukwuogo (from Awka), happened to pass by and heard me playing. He stopped and came to where I was playing music in our kitchen. I saw him and was afraid, thinking that the man was going to punish me. But the headmaster asked me to play again. I played the National Anthem and many other songs which were reigning at that time. The headmaster told me that I did not know him before, although I was in his school. He requested me to bring the xylophone to the school; I did so the next day. The teachers were all summoned and I played for them; they were all very happy. I became the school Band-Major, and led the band from 1961 - 1964 when I completed my primary school education. I naturally, suffered like any other musician. When the Nigerian civil war started, I was forced to take cover in the Cameroun. I stayed there for three years.

Before my parents took me away to the Cameroun, I joined some musicians but the band was not popular. Our instruments were even powered with batteries, not electricity. Such a band could not play in a big city like Enugu or Onitsha; even Abakaliki would have been too "civilized" for us to play in, at that time. We only played in small Nsukka villages; we did not play in Nsukka town because there were other big and better bands there. That was the type of band I first joined, and then I was in charge of the instruments. This lasted for two or more years Eventually, the members left me and I took my guitar and started learning how to play. In fact, nobody taught me how to play the guitar. I just learned through hard work and much concentration. I did not even feel the exhaustion of playing and practising alone.

Getting inspiration from a band, a particular group, an artist or somewhere else is one thing and teaching you how to play a particular instrument is another thing. I got inspiration from Congo music, but I learned their style by myself and played it on stage all alone. Nobody taught me how to do this or do that; I first learned how to play the drums and the conga, before I went on to learn how to play the bass guitar, from those instruments, I moved over to the rhythm guitar, then to the lead guitar. When I started playing the lead guitar, I started doing the vocal at the same time. I also played at Plaza Hotel in Onitsha, under my first proprietor, Mr. D. C. Onuarah, who is now dead. He owned the band and the hotel. I stayed with him for two and a half years.

After the war, around November 1971, we were to come back to Nigeria; we intended to "smuggle" ourselves into Nigeria, in order not to pass through the major road or seaport, because we had no passport. As we were in a canoe on the river, we were caught by the Camerounian seas and river guards. I could not speak French by then, but the other boys could. But because I, the leader could not speak French we were badly treated. We were taken back to the Cameroun and put into custody, put in prison. We awaited trial for three months, from November to 29 January 1971. We were finally brought to court and the judgement was passed - three months imprisonment or 30,000 francs fine. By the grace of God, Mr. Onuorah came from Nigeria and paid the fine and we were released.

When we came out, we still succeeded in "smuggling" ourselves into Nigeria. We went to Ora-Ukwu, the home of Mr. Onuorah and we stayed there for four months. We eventually signed a contract with the Plaza Hotel, Onistha. The band leader then was from the North of Cameroun; he remained in prisons because his own fine was not paid. I was made the band-leader because of my ability to communicate with the people at Onitsha and also because of what I can do in music; I play all instruments. I managed the band quite well; some of my old colleagues left and I put in new members. After some time, when these new comers have learned how to play, they leave me to be on their own. So, I continued getting new people, who altogether left after being trained.

I continued like this till late 1972 when I met Osadebe and told him that I wanted to record some music. Osadebe took me to Philips in Lagos where I made one record titled "*Onwu egbuchala anyi.*" This was my first recording ever since I started music. I did another one in "Ikom" (i.e one of the languages of Cross-River State). I then left Osadebe and went to EMI and recorded "*I no go marry my papa*" which sold so much that I had hope that one day I would really make it in music. The record was single plate which gave me my first huge money, ₦1,600.00.

I felt big by then; I did not know that I would

make such amount in my life. I took the money home to Cross River and bought a piece of land. I got little amount like ₦200, ₦300 from EMI. From the sale of that particular record, for a long time, they continued sending me money. Then, I left EMI because they no longer released my records; they refused to release my LP in 1973 titled "*Another Woman Husband*," saying that it was not good commercially. In fact, even up till 1975 they did not release that record. Then I met "Rogers All Stars," and we went to EMI and recorded "*Man don tire*" with "Rogers-All-Stars" and it did work, but EMI tried to win me back. My other records with Rogers were "Sweet Mother," "Happy Birthday," "Family Movement" etc. All of them were great hits, especially "Sweet Mother."

The first record, *"Onwu egbuchula anyi"* didn't make any good sale; it was all about death. Death is like a severe blind person who goes around touching people and whoever he touches, the person lives no more. Had it been we could see death, whenever it is coming, we would run away but since we can't, it is then certain that it will touch a person and the person will just go. I chose death as my first message in music. It was not because of the horrible experience during the civil war. Death was simply a subject that was significant among the ten songs I wrote then.

Before "Sweet Mother" was released, I first went to EMI, when Chris Nwaiga was the General Manager and EMI rejected it. I must emphasize that it was no fault of Mr. Nwaiga's; he was personally interested in it. We are still very personal good friends -Chris Nwaiga and I. Since "Sweet Mother" became globally popular, it is good to note the background to it. The present "Sweet Mother" is not the original. I composed the original "Sweet Mother" in 1974. During that time, I knew enough about night-clubs, sleep, rest, parties, etc. I was always in my room composing songs. I played and sang "Sweet Mother" with a girl who was playing at the Plaza Hotel. The girl acted as my lady vocalist. It had another beat something like rhumba, not like the present "Sweet Mother" which is much more danceable.

When I heard many records like "Super five"

reigning then, I decided to change "Sweet Mother" to a very danceable rhythm because the lyrics were for all mothers. After the composition of the current one, I kept it till 1975. I took it to EMI, they delayed it with no comments whatsoever to me. I then met Rogers. When Chris Nwaiga saw my new name, Prince Nico, he must have been confused because he knew me as Nicholas Mbarga. I started using the name, Prince Nico, because I wanted something flashy; a more musical name to match my creativity after composing so many songs.

EMI called me back, but I complained that the artist manager did not even listen to my "Sweet Mother" tape; it was just kept there with no hope of releasing it. They told me that I was probably number one or two or three on their list and should wait for some time. But, unfortunately, for them, and very fortunately, too, for me our contract had already expired.

Any way, I had the opportunity to meet any other company I liked for recording. That was when I met Rogers and discussed things with him. EMI then tried to outsmart Rogers by offering me their instruments, which were brought right down to Onitsha in complete sets. I told Rogers about it, but Rogers did not like me going back to EMI; so, the EMI instruments were rejected. Rogers took me to Lagos and from Bobby Benson we got instruments worth ₦13, 000. I never went back to EMI thus, they lost the chance of producing "Sweet Mother" to Rogers.

"Sweet Mother" later became so popular the world over, that another group, in the Caribbean did their own version of it. I am sure that the Caribbean group must have contacted "Rogers-All-Stars" and paid him to have the permission. There are about fifteen different versions of Sweet Mother: one from East Africa; one from Bocanabe; another from Cote d' Voire, a Jumbo-Caribbean disco version etc. -all as a result of the popularity of my "Sweet Mother." It played all over the world and I am sure those companies paid Rogers. If some have not done so, I can't tell, but the ones I know paid him. Some gave me credit on the sleeves of their albums, with my name as the original composer. I knew of a Kenyan band which used its own version in 1978 to compete with mine. Of course, mine was released in 1976. But Slimali, the leader of the Kenyan band behaved as if he was the original composer because he did not credit me with original composition.

Inspiration comes from here and there, from what you see every day. So, I sing about every-day-life incidents. In one of my songs "simplicity," I was saying that the God of music should help musicians to send their messages to the people. I was trying to tell my fans, the whole world, too, that what Bongos Ikwue said was right; "that what goes up must come down, that if you are to be a rich man, no matter what inflation may do, whatever happens, nothing will stop you from being what you are to be." I believe so much in destiny. That's exactly what I was trying to say in that record. Musicians are trying to make people love themselves and be happy themselves. That is exactly what I had in mind in that record. In many of my songs, if not all, I stick to my philosophy. I like to talk about day to day occurrences. In other words, I used to ask myself what the real message I have for the people is after every composition. I offer happiness and messages to the people but the messages are more important to me.

The problem in Nigeria today is that most of us leave our villages unlike our forefathers who were traditionally trained to form. Thus, the present generation is a different thing. Even before Sonny Okosun's "Which way Nigeria" was released, I did an album titled "Decency" in Paris. Because my lady singer could not sing it well, the album didn't come to Nigeria. In that song, I was talking about boys who, because they despised farm work, left their parents and relations and moved to cities looking for white collar jobs. That is a problem which particularly concerns me, every day while the number of farmers decreases (the farmers are not, numerically enough, to feed the nation), the poor quantity and quality of cash-crops contribute to inflation.

Many children go to school and when they come out from school, they go to look for white-collar jobs.

Nobody wants to help our old papas and mamas in the villages who are getting older through much hard work on the farm. We all wait for the government to provide every bit of consumer good; everybody waits for manna to fall down from heaven. When I was about to record, I went to get musicians from Kano but unfortunately, the musicians (illegal immigrants) had no papers at that time. The authorities had suspended issuing passports so I had to go alone to Paris for the recording.

Perhaps, if more Nigerian musicians put this problem more often in their messages, things will get better. In "Simplicity," I emphasized *"Cow wey no get tail."* *"Cow wey no get tail na God dey drive-am fly."* A boy who has no mother and father, or even if he has parents and there is no money; or a girl who is trying to fight to live, to make both ends meet; God would not allow difficulties to meet such helpless people or if difficulties come to them, God would help them. A poor man who is being maltreated by the rich man will have salvation in God.

We do not need songs about love now. One of the reasons for this is that even when we sang about women, we sang badly about women. I can't understand all those abuses on women. So I changed everything in favour of women, not love; and other musicians started changing too. Once something is too monotonous people become less interested but as soon as there's a change, everybody starts to enjoy the new one. "Simplicity" was made to favour them. As for pop music, disco etc., which is always "I love you, love, love, love....," I don't like it, with apologies to my fellow musicians. It looks like they don't have any other thing to sing about or any other message worth listening to. Looking at Sonny Okosun's "Which way Nigeria," it has a lot of messages, it's worth listening to because it has deep good advice which is what the country needs at this time. All these disco, pop music hardly have any message for the country, always talking about love; "I love you, you love me, my baby, my this, my that," much nonsense.

For instance, the tribes in Nigeria, what type of music can we derive from these tribes? Young musicians of present day Nigeria don't consider all these. They only succeed in playing foreign (American) music and leave our own culture at the background, in fact, it is really bad. In BBC London, I once mentioned this and the interviewer asked me if I can also play Western music, since my base is African music. I asked him why I should play Western music and which Western musicians do play African music - none. The Whiteman would not play the Blackman's music, they would never do it, why then should we play theirs? You see now that most Nigerian musicians copy white man's ways of life but you cannot get more popular than they.

Nigerian musicians can't even play their music as good as they can. It is clear that most of our musicians who started reigning from 1978 to this day are not known in US, UK or any European country, but those who made it with African music are known there because these white people are tired of their own music and so would want to know what comes from other parts of the world. Why go in to play their music which they do better than you, you can't even compete with them. Fela took up real African music and became popular world-wide. Our musicians should move back because we have musical resources yet untapped.

First of all, our T.V and Radio stations seldom project Nigerian or African artists. Most of the time, you get white men on our screen. But go to London, France etc. and you see that 99% of the artists on their screen are their own artists. They promote their own artists but here in Nigeria we have 95% foreign artists on our screens. The only way to remedy the situation is to balance the whole thing. Some countries tried to balance it with 90% their own and 10% others from other parts of the world. We say we want to Nigerianize everything but at the same time, we are taking foreign culture. You will be surprised that in the near future, some 2000 years in the future, children who will be born then will not really know what *Oji* (Kolanut) means because the traditions of the society shall have been wiped out by educated African people who would not like to have anything to do with our traditional stuff. They will thereby kill the Nigerian image, the native cultural background we have here.

If your child goes to US, to England or to Russia to study, when he comes back, let him at least know the cultural background of his people, his hometown, his state and country. Even if he won't practise his native culture, let him know it.

How would you feel if, for instance, you stayed in London for five years and came back with a white friend of yours, took him to your village and he sees you with your traditional attire, your food, etc the way you do things traditionally? Don't you know he will admire you? He surely will and will even want to copy the things he saw because they have been civilized for very many years ago, and it's going to take us quite a good number of years to be like them. That does not mean that we have to copy them, we can be developed in our way and it will be fantastic. My future plan is to go home.

I am now working on a number in Pidgin English with juju highlife music background. It's titled "*Dary ji-me*" (which means forgive me). I am going to release it soon and that's the line I want to follow - juju music in Pidgin English.

English conveys my messages down to the grassroots. Everybody, old women in the village, will understand what you are talking about, I would not like to use grammar, it's for "big men."

## Sammy Obot

"The Master at it again." Culled from *Nigerian Chronicle* and the trite-up on the sleeves of "I believe in Music."

First, it was the music, one of the tracks from his album "I believe in music" but the name didn't click. A few enquiries and I finally arrived at his State Housing Estate address where he resides with his better (socially) known brother, Chief T.A. Obot of Samesta Nigeria Limited. That's how I first met Sammy Obot (no relation of Professor Sammy Akpabot). This extremely quiet and soft-spoken musician leaves little or no lasting impression if one meets him casually for the first time, but after talking with him for about twenty minutes, one is rather very reluctant to go away because his depth of knowledge and commitment to music is, to say the least, outstanding.

His own idea of music, as can be testified to by his latest release, is not just one of those run-of-the-mill type of deafening rhythms, but disciplined, well arranged music that cuts across age or social status in tastes.

Born in Ikot Ekang in Etinan Local Government Area, Sammy Obot started his music career quite early. He played with some bands in Nigeria such as the Nigeria Police Band - 1944; Rendezvous Dance Band, Kano – 1953 and Dayspring Dance Band, Port Harcourt - 1956.

Such musical giants as late Rex Jim Lawson and late Inyang Henshaw had, at different times, played under Sammy Obot's leadership.

According to him, it was while he was with the Police Band that he taught Professor Sammy Akpabot how to play the trumpet. "I used to take my trumpet home after rehearsals and then Sammy Akpabot would come round to my house where I would show how him to play the instrument." He says he also taught Dr. Victor Olaiya how to play the trumpet.

Sammy Obot left Nigeria for Ghana where he led the Broadway Dance Band, then the leading band in that country, from 1957 to 1962.

During the visit of Queen Elizabeth II to Ghana, Sammy and his band, after a nation-wide competition, were selected to play at the reception and state ball in honour of the Queen.

It was President Kwame Nkrumah who invited Sammy to form a state band which he (Nkrumah) named "Uhuru Dance Band." Sammy built and led Uhuru from 1962 till 1965 when he left Ghana for Britain to study music at the Eric Guilder School of Music, London.

Now, Sammy Obot is back home, as he put it "to contribute my own quota towards the development of our own music."

All the songs on the six-track album were composed by Sammy Obot and arranged and produced by Jake Solo who died in a motor accident a couple of months ago.

This album, as the title implies, is a manifestation of Sammy's unflinching faith in music as a vehicle of communication and to which he is so devoted that nothing else in his life comes before music. It is indeed the result of several decades of musical experience.

**'I believe in Music'**

The long and distinguished career of Sammy Obot reflects not merely the pioneering standard of trumpet playing in Nigeria, but also the triumph of courage in the face of adversity. Sammy Obot's dedication to music is absolute; to write the history of his music career will require a whole book and this is not that book.

However, the highlights of his career include membership of the Nigeria Police Band, Lagos in 1944; from where he left to form his own band in Port Harcourt. It was while leading this band that he met late Rex Lawson and taught him how to play the trumpet. It is interesting to note that he also tutored Prof. Sam Akpabot and Dr Victor Olaiya in trumpet playing. After leading the Rendezvous Dance Band in Kano with late Inyang Henshaw as singer, Sammy Obot left Nigeria for Ghana in 1957. In Ghana, he led the Broadway Dance Band for many years; the Band won a national competition organized during the visit to Ghana, in 1961, of Queen Elizabeth II of England. After this, the late President Kwame Nkrumah of Ghana invited him to form a State House Band which Nkrumah named UHURU. After a short spell with Uhuru Band, Sammy Obot left Ghana for London. While playing in London he was studying music in Eric Guilder School of Music. Now back in Nigeria, Sammy Obot presents to the world this album, which is a result of decades of musical experience.

## Patty Obassey

> I did my primary education in my hometown -Makor in Awgu Local Government Area of Anambra State in Nigeria. I even made distinctions at that primary school level. My school was St. Theresa's Catholic School. My headmaster was one Christopher Anigbo. There was a flourishing choir for the church and I was a chorister. The choirmaster was so popular that we simply nick-named him "Choir-man." He was one Mr. Michael Awu.
>
> For my secondary education, I went to Ikom in Cross River State of Nigeria. It was known as Ikom County and it had a school band to which my cousin who took me along belonged. I learnt to play the flute there and even when I had established as a potential flutist, I never took music seriously, but I liked music a lot. I aped Congo tunes without knowing the language of its lyrics.

It was actually when I began to hear the gospel preachers, singing at crusades and camp meetings that I picked up the very first inspiration to sing. I am a Catholic adherent. I was born into Catholicism as most Nigerians are into the multi-number churches in Nigeria. So I do not believe that I should flirt with churches and denominations because as *Ndi Igbo* put it, "*ife di na be oke, di na be Ogini.*" In other words, the universality of the Church confirms that Igbo proverb "that which exists in the rats' republic also exists at Ogini's, being another kinsman's republic, too."

Sonny Oti also influenced me when he released "*Nye Ayi Miri Ndi*" -a song which was not only gospelic but also had spiritual messages. The naturality of both the lyrics and the rhythm impressed me a lot. I used to wonder when I would be in a position to do what Sonny Oti did. I admired the quality of that work but I was mainly encouraged and inspired to sing because I came to love our Lord Jesus Christ. I established a new relationship with Him. I began loving Him more than I ever did before. In an effort to praise, adore and worship Him, I discovered that I could sing and I could also play instruments to accompany any worship of Him.

I sang at church fellowships, at outdoor meetings, at camp meetings, at seminars -and all these strengthened me and my creativity. I later went overseas to Europe for further studies in Greece. My area of study was education. At Thessalonica, I studied Guidance and Counselling in Education. There, I played music during my leisure; I also became a chorister in the church where I worshipped. I also sang to entertain; I played the role of a lay-preacher as well. My inspiration mounted and grew when I came in contact with Greek songs, Spanish songs and Italian songs. Of course, Italy is the home of music and I eventually got there after two years of study in Greece. In Italy, their music gave me a lot of impetus for gospel songs. My experience there filled me up with new feelings and conviction as great artists usually n acquire.

I am a pragmatic man, I am in love with

realities, I am not a dreamer and I love moralities as well. I love to talk about God, current events in our society. I love to work with facts; all these have helped me to come to terms with a personal view about Nigeria.

We have to attack the works of the devil and devilish gang-ups. When negativism is in action, negative gang-ups must be attacked by positive gang-ups. The generation after us may be worse unless there is a balance of power brought about by godly men who are determine to do things right. Things should be done in such a way that we can regard ourselves as civilized people.

We must not allow demon-possessed and demon-influenced men and women to govern us and rule our affairs -if we do, even a little kid can predict catastrophe around the corner.

The Bible said that the pure in heart would see God. I am convinced that the man who believes in "live and let's live" will survive, but those who believe in suppression, intimidation, exploitation, lovelessness and dispassionate behaviour are barbaric. Those who live like animals cannot claim to be civilized unless they are in tune with civilization. Those who live on instinct like animals without letting nature teach them and quicken their understanding; those who deviate from nature and from the good godly system and believe in "*mago-mago*" affairs can never be creative; that is creative naturally, they can never see wisdom.

Most of our business men do not possess wisdom needed for good and real business because they possess dubious characters. Supposing our nation has developed like say, the United States of America, would our country men and women not grow up in discipline and respect for the rule of law? Would we be as unpatriotic as we are? Would we remain ignorant of the machinery of administration and even the laws of God?

Deviations result in the birth of *Ogbanje*. *Ogbanje* is a child of a deviant, it is the off-spring of a deviant, it is not in tune with creation. The Bible says that their iniquities like the wind blow them far away from God. The more they commit atrocities and iniquities, the more their iniquities scare them away from God. The farther we are from God, the more confused we are. Nigerians think they can solve their problems by getting unnecessarily sophisticated.

If all of us become dupes, there will come a point in time when there will be nothing more for us to do but to dupe or steal from amongst our corrupt body, the stolen articles which are already in circulation because there would be nobody around to be creative. Unfortunately, in our society today, if somebody is doing it right, they tag him a fool. He then becomes a drop-out in their distorted and corrupt vision. Was it not right before our eyes that rogues and highway robbers were employed as political thugs and were given cars and heavy allowances? They were also styled vanguards and youths. People won elections by giving more money to judges and we are aware of, yet nothing has been done to restore us. Nobody can support a cause he does not believe in and belief is based on understanding.

If we cannot understand the movement of a government, it will not get our support. We may pretend to belong but the actual thing is the actual will of the mind - you have to appeal to that will. That is what I am looking forward to seeing in our society for a purposeful leadership -a leadership of integrity, leadership of truth and when this happens, you will find that every youth will learn it. The majority of youths will learn it because youths learn more of what they see than what they hear. They do what others do consciously or unconsciously.

I like some crusades where people go and talk about the goodness of God. I like to see people preached to believe the gospel, instead of criticizing one church or the other. I like to go about propagating our Christian faith but I am not a fanatic.

My album "The Sower," which has the track "*Mammy-Water*" has been really successful. I thank God for it. It has created a great awareness among the youths.

Upon my return from Europe, I found out that Nigerian girls especially, were getting negatively civilized. They have been copying the lives of tramps and drop-outs and Hollywood stars from the movies they watch. They have been copying the lives of hippies. I was not happy because I know that it is not the kind of life that will lead us to the realization of desired goals. I began doing a study, was that which the youths are doing, as a result of "new wisdom" from their parents, their schools or exactly from where? I became close to some of these girls and I found out that some of them are not just negatively wise but old in evil. They have lost every sense of chastity, they say unclean things you cannot imagine a young girl would say. Then I remembered that the Bible said that they cannot blush, so they have lost that shamefacedness, they have gone into extremes.

As time went on and as I continued mingling with them, I found out that the parents of most of these girls I am talking about are in "bread" (so to speak). They are in money, so I began to study the kind of business their parents were doing, they were either some fast businessmen who were selling something or nothing at all. They were making it but they were involved in one illegal deal or the other. A lot of them belong to some secret societies, they indeed "do a lot of things" to make money.

Indeed, what the Bible said is true. "To whom you yield yourself to worship ... same will become your master." The devil is in this world to steal, to kill and to destroy. He never gives anybody any good gift without conditionalities. When people go to the demons to get money; to get extraordinary charisma for wealth, the demons try to change them, influence them and make them demonic. This he does first by leading them into some wicked acts that will severe off their existence. For instance, human sacrifice - anybody who has murdered a fellow human being has a very heavy load of guilt in his heart. He cannot see clearly. He cannot get in tune with nature without being limited by his evils.

The evil men kill other people; they kill even their own children; they eat them up to make money. How do you think such a deviant will beget a straight-forward baby? It is not possible, it is these children of deviants; children of crooks, dubious characters, murderers, sorcerers, and spiritists who become "*ogbanje.*"

Like I said in that song "*Mammy Water,*" -*ego aruru- ala, gam n'azu* (Get behind me, filthy money). I know that these evil rich men make the money in a very dubious way; and that the money they make transforms into Satan. They in turn influence our society towards evil. Because Igbo Youths like to take up challenges; they want to become as great as their fathers, ignoring the pathways of their fathers to greatness, they now run after money. Wealth has become the basis of recognition and appreciation. What the youths do to get money is incredible. Their philosophy is 'the end justifies the means.' Was it the kind of legacy their parents left for them -to jump the queue by all means. The way contemporary Igbo parents encourage their children to go into dubious means of grabbing money is by comparing them to the new money magnet status of their age-mate or one even younger in another family. These contemporary Igbo parents encourage their children to go into dubious means in acquisition of money. The youths are over-challenged and over-strained inwards with a craze for cash because when a man gets more children than he can train, he then uses the children to train himself and even to train his concubines.

Some of the children do not know that they are being used and being over-spurred. They go crazy about getting this money; and they don't have a relaxed life (I know that many among them are married to wealthy families in order to belong). They do not marry who they love and most of the time; they fall into the hands of these children of deviants: the "*ogbanje*" suitors who have no respect for the institution of marriage.

The people we call successful in our society, most of them belong to the "stained-hands" group. Their presence has contaminated our society. In turn, the right incentive to work is lacking. Even among the clergy whom we expect will become "messiahs and redeemers" or those to "redeem" us from moral decay, we are disappointed. We discover that they are just fakes; that they are merely occupational preachers. They hustle for leadership, sometimes, they even climb higher, make their way to the top and as soon as they are on top, they begin to lord it over the "called-ones" - the real shepherds who are in church; there are deviants. When Jesus saw them he questioned them angrily, "Have you people also come here to make my father's house a den of thieves." So, Christ took up the whips. I have no whip to pick up, so I have picked up the word of God. I sing it; I preach it.

Before I left for studies abroad, I participated a lot in Youths' forum on media (television and radio). My song *"Mammy Water"* was motivated by a concern for the youths. I went for further studies with this burden in my heart. I went through a lot of psychological problems which disturb the youths. I began to discover that the problems facing our youths are even more complex. They are even complicated by a lot of issues. No one wants to help the youths seriously with commitment. Generally, youths are criticized; most people hammer it down on the youths. Who bothers to worry about the problems, the cause and the effect? That motivated rather strongly my passion for educating them; it gives me an urgent sense of responsibility.

The girls, for instance, join the mammy-water cult because they need charisma to seduce men and get all the money; and ride cars even when they are not working. The rate at which they were joining the mammy-water cult alarmed me and I felt I must do something as God's servant; I had to. A necessity was laid on me, it took away sleep from my eyes. I had to do something, especially when they got to the point of snatching cars from people who were compassionate enough or lustful enough to give them lift. I knew it had reached a stage where the devil should be combated because the devil never lets go without contentions. We had to contend with the devil and recover what he has taken away from us.

When God created the world, He said, "Subdue the world, increase, multiply. Subdue the world, subdue the earth." He did not give that injunction to the demon. It was to us; we human beings are God's image. So, His will has to be done here on earth as it is in heaven. Why should we give the devil all the chance?

Look at how they raped us during the political elections of our country; look at how they raped our government; look at how they raped our society and pursued us into the kitchen, disgracing us and robbing us of our integrity and greatness. We were dumbfounded, so we kept quiet. We noticed moral cowardice everywhere. Even those who knew the truth refused to say it because they were afraid to die, yet the sooner we die, the longer we reach the stage of immortality if our hands are clean. Why should we be afraid of death?

Some people had a fantastic idea about the mermaid. They say she gives money, charisma, beauty and all that. Actually, Lucifer was beautiful; his descendants should be beautiful. Because they worship the demon, they visualize the demon even when they are making love because the demon makes love to them. The demon affects the child they beget; it affects the child's brain, the genes, the colour, everything; that which they communicated in spirit, now affects the physical. When you see the beauty of the mermaid, it is definitely alluring and seductive; but anyone who is spiritual will know that it is the beauty of the demon. Anybody who is spiritual knows the riches of the demon.

I don't feel that I can, at any time, succumb to bargain with the devil. I will always do what Jesus Christ did. He said, "Get thee behind me, Satan." I have no time to bargain with the devil and I will like our society to do the same - to stop bargaining with the devil. He is an old crook, in fact the oldest roving crook. Before man was created, Satan already existed. He knows a variety of tricks - so if you want to eat with him, you need a long spoon.

Consider a number of prayer houses. They shout God! God! Jesus! Jesus! Yet they communicate with the demons. A lot of people have been with these prayer houses over the years but rather than know

God, it is the devil they have been worshipping. People should stay away from the Devil. He is a politician and a diplomat.

The source of power is God. We must look before we leap. The devil sometimes fulfils his promises in order to steal his client's (a man's) conscience. He would use a man to any extent. Thus, I appeal to our youths to stop imitating or copying what they do not fully understand; to be themselves always for that is the only way to be really creative and original -to be pragmatic. Let us not live like dangling participles; let us pitch our tent somewhere, have a background and origin.

Look at our marriage institutions; we do not marry for love but for lust. We are ruled by a lust for beauty and a lust for materialism. We confuse the L for Love with the L for Lust.

The Church itself compounds the problem by introducing a marriage culture that is not derived from practical experience in African culture. The Church instead of healing this world of lack of rapport between the spouses increases it through hypocrisy. This the church did by establishing a standard they know nobody can really in all honesty live up to in marriage. Those who tried to live up to it acquired complex problems. Thus, it is proper for us to face the question of marriage with integrity: fall in love, engage, court and marry. Not marriage before love because we do not pass through the honest convention; our children are usually born as loveless creatures -delinquent and revengeful. They avenge their lovelessness on the society. Nobody seems to have the time to give them love because the marriage which brought them forth into the world was a mere contract.

# 5

# Jottings from the Author's diary

This addendum is drawn mainly from my "mental archives," If I may borrow Carlos Moore's phrase: "mental archives." For me, this book has been a project 1 set for myself in order to erect a monument in memory of my very dear friends who are now of blessed memory: Rex Lawson, Celestine Ukwu, Dansatch Ayo of Jos and to honour one I respect, the late Uncle Bobby Benson. It is also to honour those alive because an Igbo proverb says "The more you praise an action-man, the more active he becomes."

In this connection, I wish to document my relationship with a number of musicians. Such a relationship had placed me in an advantaged position which profoundly complemented my researches. It also gave my field assistants an easy access to these celebrities. Sometimes, some musicians would refuse to talk to my field assistants because they felt a physical re-union with me was dearer to their hearts. There are also some of them who believe that I am a "legendary artiste," they would rather use that opportunity to meet me formally for the first time. At such meetings, I was usually lavishly entertained.

I know that a book of this nature would suffer defects of all sorts. While I submit to the indifference of some critics and recognize their treasure of knowledge in this area of study, I make no apologies for any loopholes or inadequacies because, by this work, I have partly succeeded to satisfy some personal goals discussed earlier on.

As an "occasional musician," I am very intimate with many Nigerian Stars. As a deputy Sigma Chief, in the early sixties, my opinion was respected by the Sigma Club in the selection of dance bands. "Installation Calypso", my first single, was released on Phillip's West Africa Records in 1963. It was also honoured by the World University

Service in Geneva in 1965. I have had access to most musicians in their early "experimental" days. That was why, in 1980, my chat with Fela Anikulapo-Kuti was a "nostalgic" get-together.
Sonny Okosun used to address me as "Uncle." He solicited for "Togetherness" with his lyrics and later asked the kind of question one would expect from a patriot, with his song-text, "Which Way Nigeria." I myself had positively affirmed even before his skepticism that "Nigeria Go Survive." Throughout the night of 1983 Presidential Election, his 'Togetherness" and my "Nigeria Go Survive" alternated on National Television Authority's network till dawn. Part of my lyrics reads:

> Nigeria Go Survive
> Africa go survive
> Black people go survive
> Nigeria go survive
> Nigeria no go surrender
> Africa go be one
> Black people go unite
> Blood is thicker than water

It was Jake Solo who, in 1983, engineered the recording of the above L.P at Tabansi in Onitsha. My producer and label-owner was Chris Nwaiga who was the general manager of EMI in Nigeria for a number of years. In 1970, Jake Solo had played the bass guitar while backing me vocally e.g. during the recording of my "*kosi Nwam*" extended plays which brought my songs-of-the-war-years together on an album on Phillips West Africa Records label.

In the early sixties, Agu Norris threw a joke at me, "I was told that whenever I meet you, I will see my image as if before a dressing mirror." That was in Lagos; at that time, his song-text in Yoruba language "*Ntori Kini, ntori awa-wa*" was a sensation. That, too, was the period when Kakadu Night Club was an inter-racial spot, as popular as Bobby Benson's Caban Bamboo. I watched Victor Uwaifo first at K.K.D. and E. C. Arinze's guitarist singing an Edo language song written by him.

I met Roy Chicago when I was preparing the record "*Omenali*" in 1974. He arranged my contact with *Monomono* to back me.

In a write-up on the release of an album by this author mentioned above, which was captioned "*Omenali*" (i.e. Tradition) on the label of phonogram (Phillips) in 1974, Dr. Ayo Mamudu observes:

> The tapestry of the tunes ...
> an approach which underlines

> his attachment to folklore...there is
> nostalgic for the poetry
> of moonlit scenes of story telling in the village...
> Although his interest is mostly engaged with the
> beauties, subjects and methods of folklore, he is
> also alive to the realities
> and issues dour times as in "Black Fellowship"
> and "Memories of Leads" ... His tunes may recall
> choral singing and the spirituals but they are
> based, in the main, on the simple, gentle rhythms
> of the highlife of the 1950s.
> Thus they may be rather listened to...

I. K Dairo (Member of the British Empire) was the top juju band in the mid-sixties. It took him a few minutes to adapt the Igbo songs I wrote, for one of Nigeria's Dakar festival plays, to juju music. At Dakar, he and his band orchestrated while I sang my songs at the party held for the Nigerian Festival Theatre Company by the Nigerian Ambassador at Dakar, the Senegalese Capital, during the First World Negro Arts Festival.

Bongos Ikwue, Nigeria's "country-music" star, received me at his Lagos Tin-Can Island home for a chat on this study. In 1980, Zeal Onyia gave me a prestigious ride in his Mercedez-Benz, to his residence in Surulere, in Lagos, where I recorded his views and mini-biography. The late gentlemen Celestine Ukwu offered me the first gift of Jl (One pound), after the civil war, at Enugu, and invited me to see him play at Enugu Recreation Club. I did, in the company of a budding star, Nellie Uchendu and her sister, in 1970. Nellie Uchendu is now a Nigerian star. One of the songs which brought her further up into limelight was "Late Nite Husband" written by me. I wrote the lyrics and slotted it into Israel Nwoba's rhythm of the fifties named "Money Palavar."

Bola Johnson and His "Easy Life Top Beats" based at Mokola in Ibadan did the instrumental backing of my first single mentioned earlier on. Orlando Julius backed my second single which was reviewed by Tony Amadi and captioned "Those swinging egg-heads" in the defunct *Morning Post* newspaper in 1966, the title was "Foundation for Posterity."

Bala Miller & His African Pyramid was, and has been, responsible for the greatest publicity given to my album, "Late Nite Husband." Paulson Kalu announced at the elitist Umuahia Ritz Club, in 1982, that my music inspired him significantly (he meant my song-texts). Among my song-texts which were inspirational to him was "*Ilu Ndi Igbo*" (proverbs of *Ndi Igbo*).

Rex Lawson was very close to me from 1963 until 1966 when the Nigerian civil war cut off our contact. I had fulfilled my promise to bring him over from Maryland Hotel, Port Harcourt, to play for Sigma Club in 1964. That he played as number one dance band at the Sigma carnival has been recorded earlier on. I had visited Rex Lawson's home at Buguma. I cannot forget that ride in the "outboard-engine boat" in the company of a kind volunteer guide, Miss Caroline Wokoma, a staff of African Continental Bank at Port Harcourt, who was going home to spend her weekend. I got to Buguma and that was the home of the legendary Rex Lawson; Mr. Chamberline Oyibo played host. Rex Lawson was in his Owerri Road residence at Mile One Diobu in Port Harcourt. When I took the outboard-engine-boat again, it was to Abonema as guest of G.F.S Harrison who actually "introduced" Rex Lawson to me. Both Chamberline and Faye (G.F.S) were not only friends of mine; they also shared Mellanby Hall students' residence with me at Ibadan University. As my friendship with Rex Lawson grew, and as I re-exposed him to Ibadan and Lagos, he quit Maryland Hotel, but left a eulogy for the Nnewi-businessman, Mr. Udeaja, who owned Maryland. The song was "*Aye Muba Udeaja.*"

Rex Lawson returned to Lagos which was his old home in the music business. Rex Lawson was fond of the song-text I produced to honour Dick Tiger after his middleweight title fight with Gene Fullmer at the Liberty Stadium, Ibadan. The title of the song was "Dick Tiger," also on Phillip's label.

For Goethe Institute in Lagos, I starred in the documentary film "Saturday in Lagos" directed by Klaus Stephen. The song I wrote for the film was "Lagos Calypso." King Kennytone & His Western Top Toppers backed me in spite of his craze for Twist.

Inyang Henshaw established a relationship with me in 1963 inside the studios of Phillips West African Records Company at Ijora, in Lagos, because I satisfactorily explained how I got at the Efik song "*Sona Da K' usen ikpe*" which would be the flipside of "Installation calypso". I mentioned White Star Choral Party of Calabar, Ambo Line's name, and the label "Patsol" (coined from the label owner, Patrick Solomon - a Lebanese merchant who later became a Nigerian and a Chief at Calabar). The late Chief Patrick Solomon also owned a movie house named Patsol Cinema. I grew up as a kid in Calabar and I am fluent in Efik language. Inyang Henshaw smiled when he heard that and from then on our chat was in Efik. He was, at that time, designated Talent Scout of Phillips West Africa Records.

Eddie Okonta was the only one who offered "Paradise" here upon earth because he directed the resident band at Paradise Hotel, Ibadan, even on Sundays. It was my responsibility to contract him for Students Union Rag-Day Shows and their defunct Panorama Dance for freshmen.

The reception Victor Uwaifo gave me in his home in Benin City sometime in 1979 was great. I had arrived late in Benin City that night, checked into a hotel and rode to his *Joromi* Hotel. He was just back from Lagos but that did not bother him. He guided me to his home which is really the handiwork of a house designed by an architect for himself. The mural paintings were great. We stayed late at the private bar in his home. My friend, Mustapha, and my niece, Lovina, enjoyed Victor's company. He offered me a complimentary copy of his autobiography with the title: "My Life."

Earlier on in Jos, by early seventies, Victor Uwaifo had cancelled his earlier decision not to play for a television programme, "Saturday Serenade" produced and directed by Dele Angulu. He did not associate me with the programme until Dele asked me to intervene. Victor would not play because the fees were unattractive. I was the guest presenter of that popular programme on Benue - Plateau Television at Jos. Victor accepted the poor fees because of me; when I talked to him at Terminus Hotel, Jos. Dele Angulu was happy.

The day that crowned it all for me was the day Sam Akpabot, Zeal Onyia and myself were guests to Bala Miller at the Costain Club in Kaduna. I did the vocal for "*Late Nite Husband*". Zeal Onyia recreated Louis Satchmo Armstrong with the trumpet and sang "*Vic, nyem a fumo.*" Sam Akpabot gave jokes and songs and recalled those "All Stars Days" of his evergreens.

I was virtually Sonny Okosun's guest at Gondola Night Club in Lagos. Power Mike -the undefeated wrestling champion or Mike Okpala, also met me for the first time that night. I had just completed a recording at EMI backed by the Gondoliers, in memory of the late Onyekozuru Chukwumerije - a graduate of the University of Nigeria, Nsukka, and a wonderful young man who stayed close to me during the Nigerian Civil War years. His brother, Uche Chukwumerije, was the sponsor of the recording and I was in the home of the Gondoliers that night.

Dan Satch Ayo was the leader of the "Sahara All Stars" at Jos. He was the leader of the resident band of Havana Nite Club at Jos. In the early seventies and before Dan Satch Ayo died, I was always a guest-singer during their "Ladies Night." But suddenly Dan Satch Ayo was no more and that was the night he and Bongos Ikwue featured as supporting bands before Jimmy Cliff took the floor at the Rock Garden of Plateau Hotel in Jos. As a round of applause greeted the end of Ayo's band show, he collapsed, and was rushed to the hospital where he died.

The day I saw Chris Ajilo again in February, 1985, at his office in Polygram Records Limited, Lagos, our emotional hug cancelled more than one decade which separated those years of regular get-together and the present.

Any time I play back "*Atabala* Woman" by "Professional Seagulls," my mind settles on some of its musicians with whom I had shared good times when they made good music in Rex Lawson's band. And somehow, whenever I have a flash of the Professional Seagulls in Port Harcourt, on my mind, I recall Chuks Nwamama who, when he was alive, made his highlife popular with his "*Chuks ebulu egwu we laba Pitakwa* (Port Harcourt)" and Eddie Okwedi whose music the "popular women" of Bonny Street, in Port Harcourt, loved in the mid sixties, and the late Chief Bill Friday, a musical link between Nigerian and Ghanaian highlife - the fallen stars, left their foot print on the sands of time.

Rex Lawson's childhood was the forerunner of the great man who would emerge from an "*abiku*. As I sat down writing and listening to local radio programmes functional to this work, a voice came over ABS (Anambra Broadcasting Service) Radio One, Enugu. One of Rex Lawson's classics came serenading. The programme was "Tribute to Fallen Stars." As the track faded, the voice of the producer, Ejike Amadi, came loud and clear:

> Rex Lawson was born on 4 March, 1935.
> He was the 4th child of his parents.
> His mother, Christiana was a native of Owerri...
> Three children were born before him...

The producer went onto comment on the first three children believed to be *ogbanje* or *abiku*. Each died early in life at some point. When Rex came, it was obvious that he was also an "*ogbanje*." On his little body was a machete-cut scar to identify him as an *abiku*. He was also infested with small pox and was so sickly that his mother had to take him to all sorts of medicine men beyond his Kalabari home. His father naturally lost interest because it appeared to him that Rex would also die like the three before him.

While at school, Rex Lawson sued his father to court for neglect. He won the case, but his father was furious; he cursed Rex. He was thus cut-off from his father until his debut with his first disc "*Tamuno Bo Ibroma*" - a disc which heralded the entry of a famous son into the world of Nigerian music celebrities.

Rex was originally named James Osima Lawson. By the time of his death, his Mayors Band was re-named "Cardinal Rex Jim Lawson and His Rivers-Men." That was obviously his reaction to the effects of the Nigerian Civil War. He probably meant to identify himself more openly with his father's homeland. That way, his contributions to Kalahari literature, culture, history and image were unequivocally backed by his homeland base.

Rex served as second trumpeter under "Lord Eddison" at Port Harcourt. Sammy Obot, who was first trumpeter, actually served as Rex Lawson's tutor. Sammy Obot later went to Ghana and led the Professional Uhuru Dance Band, while Rex left Port Harcourt to work with a number of popular bandleaders: Bobby Benson, Victor Olaiya, Chris Ajilo and Roy Chicago in Lagos.

James Osima Lawson, after what might be called a working or advanced apprenticeship in Lagos, returned to the defunct Eastern Nigeria. At Onitsha, Nigerphone Studios and Onitsha's fans would be Rex's catapulting base to stardom. He played every evening at Mayors Hotel. His music had a spiritual atmosphere and gospel trait. Fans quickly tagged the shows as -evenings of worship with the Pastor. Thus Rex was "ordained Pastor" by his fans. His name got the title Pastor Rex Jim Lawson. He was by now also crowned king of highlife which explains the place of the name Rex in his new titles.

His popularity spread and was accompanied by demands for tours. After a show at Aba, fans "promoted him to the higher clerical office of Bishop." He later became "Archbishop" and finally they still thought that only the heights were good enough for a man who had lifted highlife into the realm of beauty and excellence. He was ordained "Cardinal."

He was not just a moving composer, singer, instrumentalist, arranger and band leader; he also introduced the bongos drum and the wind instrument "sax" to Nigerian highlife.

During the Nigerian Civil War, he became a captain, directing the band of the Third Marine Commando, of the Nigerian Armed Forces.

"Tributes to Fallen Stars" observed that Cardinal Rex Lawson, after the War, discovered that he needed to rename his dance-band. He dropped "Rivers-men" and did yet another christening of his band. He signed a contract with Phillips Recording Company and recorded "*Tamuno Bo Ibroma*" for the third time until "*Iworiwo Iriworiwomma*" was popularized.

Rex continued his communal living and "sharing" with his colleagues; he shared sleeping accommodation with them; he shared the seats of their bus transport with them during every show tour. As one critic put it, "his popularity never 'ruled' his head; nor did it mar a healthy relationship with his employees." He always shied away from the frontline on which his ingenuity had placed him. When at last he wrote a song-text which could be regarded as a eulogy for himself in 1970, it was still typically about the modest Rex Jim Lawson. In that song-text, he looked at himself as "music personified" and as "god of music." Still he gave an undisputed first position to God, the creator, who gave him the talent and gift of music. He emphasized that he needed no charm to be a popular music luminary. It was God who sent him into the world to make music.

By the end of 1970, the first incident which would give a hint to confirm what his father suspected in his childhood happened. His father, when Rex was a baby, had dumped him in a bush to forestall his fears that Rex was an *ogbanje*. Also, small pox, at that time, was still not quite lifted from "a traditional evil-forest disease."

By 1970, he was already a highlife superstar; was that why his latest disc bore his real name "Osima" in its title? Why was he asking for a helping hand in that song-text? Why was he calling on mankind to help? "Brothers and Kinsmen, help!" Was danger around the corner? Was he a visionary or was it the characteristic self destruction and personal doomsday prophecy of the *abiku*?

For the first time, Rex threw away his communal affinity with his colleagues. He let them go ahead of him to Warri to "Warm up" before his arrival for a show. He tried to collect a new private car he had paid for at Port Harcourt. The car was not ready for delivery, since he had to catch up with the show at Warri, he hired a car at Port Harcourt and drove it. At Effurun, on the outskirts of Warri, his car crashed, that accident took Rex's life.

It was a personal loss to me. No tribute to Rex Lawson could please me more than that by E.T. Mensah. In 1984, his interview in Lagos with the *National Concord* (a Nigerian daily) was in my view, a score board for the pioneers of Nigerian highlife. E.T. Mensah rated Rex Lawson as a "younger contemporary" of Bobby Benson's, in whose hand highlife was a serious art created with aesthetic beauty.

I have never met G.T. Onwuka personally and yet he is one of the great names of highlife music in Nigeria but I do recall that he was a resident band to Biafran BOFF organization during the Nigerian Civil War. He was based at Okagwe in Ohafia near my own hometown, Arochukwu.

It appears that a rise regenerates from a fall. As I mourn the demise of Rex Lawson, Celestine Ukwu and Dan Satch Ayo of Jos, new stars, emerge to keep the touch of continuity afloat.

I was rehearsing for an experimental recording as part of my lab work for this book when the arrival of Patty Obassey was announced. We were sharing the same drummer. Patty had a show at Ihiala in Anambra State in Nigeria on the previous evening. I thought I was a stranger to the young gospel highlife musician who has just joined Nigerian stardom with his album, "The Sower." Patty said, "After the Civil War, when I heard your music on Phillips entitled "*Nye Ayi Miri Ndu*" (Give us, oh, Lord, the water of life), in 1971, 1 said to myself, is it possible for me to sing like him one day?" Today, Patty Obassey is popular with the release of every new album of satirical and witty songtexts.

Contact with musicians is contact with new dimensions in understanding the minds of a corpus of artists who have remained an enigma to the society since the genesis of city popular music.

# 6

# Concluding observations

The "scapegoat culture" which blames national and group, as well as individual misfortunes and disasters on external forces is not a new phenomenon. Big Powers use the scapegoat culture, at ideological level, in world politics. Victims of colonialism and apartheid exploit it whenever their political, social, cultural and economic boat flounders. Thus, if in an attempt to conclude this work, the scapegoat culture is made functional, the unprejudiced merit of it should be seen as significant.

As a popular music genre, highlife has been established from the early fifties, as an important African institution on the West Coast of Africa in both Anglophone and Francophone countries. Highlife is in no way "a fading fad" for, rather than fade, it has continued to metamorphose into new forms held firmly on the same modern traditionalized base. Its survival has been guaranteed by succeeding musicians who have developed new forms which they, unwittingly, do not credit to highlife for fear of being dropped from the "chart" manipulated by western music technology critics. Most Africa experiments, including the art of nation building, collapse partly because their indigenous architects allow foreign critics to shepherd them into declaring the experiments as impotent, primitive and incapable of "civilized" results.

As soon as an African institution passes through the crucible of accepted growth process, Western critics' nuclear warhead artilleries would make it their target and testing ground until unprejudiced Western scholars join African nationalists in defending it; and such Western scholars never really succeed unless they emphasize the excellence of primitivity, exorcism and the exotic. If the collapse of such an institution cannot be brought about directly by foreign manipulators, it comes to fruition through their local brainwashed Africans. A victim of the brainwashing institution is hardly aware that he is an alumnus and victim. He is usually as sensitive as the "mentally deranged" who keeps saying "I know what I am doing."

It is not the foreign critic who tagged highlife "a fading fad," it is some indigenous critics who did. Some of the write-ups seem to indicate prejudice and hero-worship. Some merely sound as the voice of the unprivileged mob; that is why Victor Olaiya, one of the most respected pioneers of highlife music in Nigeria blamed indigenous disc jockeys and music journalists. He attacked them in a fit of emotion: "They project foreign music more than our own indigenous music." Dr. Olaiya observes, "these new contemporary sounds must have to borrow something from highlife to be able to stay ... Even 'Fuji' is returning to Highlife."

Fuji is not actually returning to highlife, it is one of the branches of highlife; although it is an off-shoot of juju music. Through Ebenezer Obey, the rhythm and style of highlife was absorbed into juju music. Absorption of foreign culture is one of the attributes of growth, thus, one cannot agree with Dr. Olaiya's views that there is no "foreign music influence." There is nothing wrong with "foreign influence" once it is "universalized." In fact, although Dr. Olaiya rightly pointed out that "you can play highlife without Western instruments," he also admits "we are only giving it a new face by bringing the westernized instruments like horn and guitar." Yet, Victor Olaiya claims that it was he who introduced the Yoruba "talking drum into highlife in 1956 through the number '*Aiye Omuti*" which also as a coincidence covered the year "he played a nation-wide tour during the visit of Queen Elizabeth II of England to Nigeria in 1956."

Highlife exposed itself to Western technology culture right from its beginning in the early fifties. Bobby Benson, as early as 1947/48, had upon his return, introduced western electronic gadgets like guitar to West African urban music. By the time E.T Mensah recorded his first highlife music comprising "*Esi Nana*," "*Nke-bo-baya*" and "All for you" -all the disc were popular in West African, Western electronic instruments were already in circulation. Because highlife was born into urban setting, it started fulfilling that scientific condition of growth right from birth. What existed before 1951 was really not aesthetically highlife in all its forms until E.T. Mensah "started to dress it up by harmonizing it and adding a touch to the arrangement with bongos, claves, conga, marracas, jazz-drums; all assembled to give a pattern of music." He "allowed the music to be led by wind instruments like trumpet."

## Concluding observations

To continue the demands of growth, highlife interacted with foreign culture by its use of the verbal language of communication, in its song-texts, which would be understood by a greater population of the world. Those two are English and French which still act as the lingua franca in West Africa. This did not compromise the role of indigenous African languages to project African culture. Highlife also succeeded to recycle foreign "beats and rhythms" which originated from Africa as well as retaining some archetypal and prototype forms which are still functional and extant.

Some Western critics do not see some African institutions as possessing the dynamics and potentialities for civilized development. Thus when Fela Anikulapo Kuti develops highlife to a revolutionary stage tagged "Afro-beat", western critics which had earlier credited its innovative contribution, refuse to see it as an off-spring of highlife and share his "anti-colonialism visions and crusade." It is not even easy for the youths to understand why ageing E. T. Mensah of Ghana who was as popular, between early fifties and sixties, as Bob Marley, later has been on a campaign to monumentalize highlife.

E. T. Mensah's first choice, for a joint album of "Evergreens," was naturally Victor Olaiya of Nigeria. If Rex Lawson were alive, he would either share that first choice or voluntarily drop to second position, as a mark of respect for Victor Olaiya, who was awarded an honorary doctorate degree at Prague in Czechoslovakia during the First Jazz International Festival where he succeeded to incorporate "Western musical instruments with African instruments to play jazz."

In terms of refinement and excellence in the art of highlife music, Nigerian Rex Lawson (of blessed memory) is E.T. Mensah's counterpart at the "classical level."

E.T. Mensah hopes to do joint albums with two other popular Nigerian musicians: Bala Miller and Victor Uwaifo. The two names are not only well established in Ghana and African music world, both are, in fact, connected with Ghana by marriage.

Highlife is one of the emblems of African cultural and political identity. Highlife, kolanuts and palm-wine are "nostalgic forces" in the West, particularly in the United States of America; and this is probably as a result of the popularity of novels by writers like Chinua Achebe and Amos Tutuola as well as the works of play-wrights like Wole Soyinka and scholars like Professor H.N. Nketia of Ghana.

I recall that in 1980, I was guest at a birthday party being hosted by a young Nigerian student in Sacramento, the humble State Capital of elegant California in United States of America. I had just completed four runs of a drama production. My host, upon my request, approved that I should bring along the Black Americans who comprised the cast of my show. They looked forward to three events at the party: the opportunity to learn and dance highlife; participate in the ceremony of pouring libation with palm-wine and of invocations which precede the breaking of kolanuts. Of course, this event took place when I was an "old creation." What they would miss was the palm-wine because there was none around but there was kolanut. I went along to the party with Nigeria's Chris Okotie's Western pop album which even caused some Nigerian housewives to break a taboo because they enrolled as "members of Chris Okotie's fan club." The album was, of course, "I need someone." I also had the popular highlife album of Ikenga superstars as well as Prince Nico's "Sweet Mother".

Our Nigerian host tried toasting with Californian champagne; the Black Americans, and even the Whites in the party, protested. Palm-wine was the answer but there was none so, they were contented, in spite of feeling disappointed. 1 was called upon to perform the ceremony and kolanut was passed around. When it was dance time, the Nigerians jumped for Chris Okotie's number. The Americans demanded highlife music and "Ikenga Super Star." The apartment floor was crowded with dancers; it was followed by Nico Mgbarga, then a chain of Fela's music. In quick succession, the music of Sunny Ade, Ebenezer Obey and Rex Lawson dominated the scene till the party was over in the early hours of the morning.

At the drum-room (night club) of Hotel Presidential in Enugu, Nigeria, a group of touring Europeans was neither moved to the dancing floor by the live reproduction of Michael Jackson's number nor those of Abba, Stevie Wonder, New Edition, Boney M and Musical Youths. E.O Arinze's resident band (E.O Arinze was not around) felt uncomfortable because of the reaction of the white "guests." The band had played what they did all along to impress the Europeans, then they struck a highlife number. First to arrive on the dancing floor were the foreigners and as they clapped, hopped and danced in and out of rhythm, the American among them went up to shake hands with the musicians saying "I don't want no bullshit copy-cat thing...highlife is beautiful...beautiful, men... sure, I dig it."

In food culture, there are the Chinese with their chopsticks, the Italian with their spaghetti, the Irish with their potato, the Yorkshire-English with their pudding, the Japanese with their raw fresh fish. If the African's pounded cassava *foo-foo*, which demands washing of hands, and drying with fresh napkin, appeared on an international menu table, it has to be tagged "exotic" and would need a syndicate of public relations agents to convince Africans themselves to identify with it before the "civilized" world.

What has kept academics like Professor Samuel Akpabot, whose band, "Samuel Akpabot All Stars Band" which was among the already operational band of the late forties, from identifying with the development of highlife, is evidently the fact that highlife has remained a factory of sheer talents. Thus, one cannot agree with Victor Olaiya that "you don't have to go to a dancing school to learn how to dance highlife," yet he adds: "it has some very peculiar beat and tempo, highly rhythmic beat peculiar to African rhythm." While it took the early years to establish identifiable rhythm known as highlife, nothing further was done to agree on uniformed elements and professional characteristics. It is that loophole of "spontaneity" that has left it as a dumping ground for adventurers.

To become what he is now in music, Fela Anikulapo-Kuti spent four and half years at Trinity College of Music in London, studying classical music. Does that not explain why his 'wedding,' of his original African rhythms, to his militant and satirical song-texts has a universally accepted texture? A number of Ghanaian bands also started reading music in the early years of highlife. Thus, the need for a formal education in music must be emphasized. Career musicians who later had the opportunity at any level are happy they did. E.O Arinze had already become popular before he became a part-time student of Steve Rhodes, when Steve Rhodes directed the Nigerian Broadcasting Service Band-stand on air. Bala Miller has continued to advocate the need for formal education in music; at least so that illiterate or half-literate musicians may snatch some elementary theories needed in understanding music.

Although there is evidence of inadequacies in theory orientation in African highlife, yet as the years passed by, lyrics of highlife grew in subtlety, wit, effrontery, propaganda for the protection of the society, as well as confrontation with the establishment, until musicians levelled up with the press. But while the press does not quite have an alternative to communicating the naked truth without a veil, the press still has a greater risk orientation. One is aware, of course, that the press can no longer be credited with "unadulterated truth" given a choice between patriotism, nationalism, individual interest and truth.

It is not in the best interest of the musician or the society to mount a permanent antagonistic stance against any and every establishment. Musicians should not constitute themselves into an opposition party but into a propelling force which may examine critically the efforts of the establishment and help to redirect the authorities towards popular goal-oriented ends. In other words, messages in the song-texts should be seen as complementary efforts by musicians towards nation building. It is not healthy or pragmatic to expect that an ideal society can be established anywhere in the world. No government can really buy anti-colonialism slogan wholesale because no nation can exist in isolation. Without diplomatic relationships even with enemy states, governments cannot really operate effectively. Thus, musicians, like society, have to criticize the system reasonably in order to win the support of those they are supposed to protect. A revolution, in any form, has to show evidence that a system has so completely decayed and become decadent that a total cancellation of that system is the only answer. A revolution also has to show that the admiration it wins from foreigners cannot be interpreted at home as an act of sabotage; and it also has to convince the home front hat it is guided by sanity.

Once you start a revolution, you are a potential leader; and no matter how we look at it, leadership must show qualities which can conform to what the society regards as their moral values. Such moral values and ethics also have to create a place for interaction with external values. Thus, while song-texts can identify the musician as a nationalist, Pan-Africanist and rebel, the society monitors the judicious use of such lyrics.

Time factor, the mood of the society, the human elements and flexibility in the operation of results of visions; unless they are brought to interact with dynamism, spills over into the realm of lawlessness. Not even rebellion or revolution can function without an accepted code of conduct or discipline. Probably, an "outlaw" revolution may catch up as fire producing an external leadership.

In Nigeria, Fela Anikulapo-Kuti had made it clear that he was not really interested in Presidency and political leadership. In other words, he was only concerned in creating a revolutionary political awareness with his song-texts. His lyrics are indisputably excellent examples of nightclub rhetoric. His lyrics also represent political campaign manifestos. In Fela's music, his innovative rhythm and sound merely play the role of a backing power.

There is no doubt that Nigeria is peopled by an alert indigenous population very strongly committed to "native democracy." Even under a military regime, Nigerians are fearlessly vocal and critical. Nigerians are also aware that even the Armed Forces are not ghosts but Nigerians evenly represented in the Nigerian military world. The Nigerian Armed Forces are also aware of that, thus they are sensitive to the wishes of the people, although they rigidly try to draw a line between characteristic army discipline target and indiscipline. Such military stance is what the civilian world sometimes refers to as "their insensitivity."

Because Fela Anikulapo-Kuti has remained as militant as the army, conflict and confrontation have always been inevitable. Fela in reference to his "Kalakuta Republic" disaster indirectly confirmed the sensitivity of the Nigerian Army to the voice of its civilian public when he said that his lawyer did not want to tell him that "they wanted to settle;" that his lawyer wanted court action for the selfish reasons of making a name for himself. "They wanted to settle" was a direct reference to the military government of his country at that time. In spite of his album "Zombie" and all that conflict, the Nigerian Army is too civilized to be involved in antagonizing a popular indigenous critic indiscriminately. Fela's records were played by quite a number of the rank and file in their homes. Some of their children were also Fela's fans. His popularity in Nigeria had risen astronomically to the point that the youths excitedly discussed his intention to run for Presidency. As Nigerian citizens, in military uniform, soldiers do not "hate" Fela.

It was the twenty-seven-wives incident that "crushed" Fela in Nigeria. It meant that he now stepped on the toes of the people he was "committed to protect." The girls were teenagers; most of them were still at school. But it is significant to note that they escaped from their home voluntarily for a future with Fela.

Parents and guardians who knew the Christian background of Fela were shocked, but because of their guarded respect for Fela's effrontery, they did not go to court because every new album of Fela brought new discourse projecting his patriotism, nationalism, Pan Africanism, etc., in conflict with his moral demeanour as a responsible Nigerian citizen. Most parents of Fela's queens would never have cared about his lawyer's fear of bigamy since they would rather protect their daughters and wards for the sake of family names. If Fela had attempted to go through customary marriage negotiation with the parents and guardians of his queens, he would have established a recorded evidence of his respect for traditional marriage laws. Practically, most parents would not stand Fela's proposals, if he did. That, in itself, would have increased Fela's fans and follower-ship. In Nigeria, every daughter being proposed to is a potential insurance, one way or other, for his parents or guardians. It was not judicious to be in conflict with both the society from whom you drew your support at the same time as the establishment. Even if they mandated you formally, as their mouthpiece, they would withdraw that mandate on the spot.

But equally unpublicized is the fact that these girls voluntarily escaped from their homes to seek employment in Fela's popular and compelling Afro-beat.

Their relationship started first as employer and employee contract. But then urban popular music is still not a popular career in Nigeria. It is suspected as a vocation which exposes girls to prostitution. As a professional musician, Fela would want to break that primitive "taboo." Yet the soldiers' brutality on the girls during the "Kalakuta Republic Sack" was an eloquence of public disapproval of the uncultural behaviour of the girls who did not bow to traditional feminine decorum. But then, in Fela's favour is the fact that in the case of a judge's daughter, Fela insisted that the girl, instead of taking shelter in his home, should go and plead with her uncle to intervene and get reconciled to her father. When the girl insisted she would not return to her home that very night, Fela in sympathy, sent her to be accommodated in the family home of his friend.

Fela Anikulapo-Kuti is very central to any discussion on African music song-texts in any meaningful study in that area. No study can defocus his most outstanding contributions, through music, to the development and image of the African and the Blackman in world politics and their struggle for racial survival. A jail house or prison is not a resort for holidaying. Neither is a police baton, when used as a riot-weapon, a plaything. Many do not wish that Fela disappears, as Carlos Moore perceived; many would rather wish to recall the very utterance of Right Reverend Israel Oludotun Ransome Kuti's concern for his third child, Fela, when that devout Christian said to his wife, Fela's mother, "with what we know about him, was it not our duty to inculcate in him a sense of caution to restrain his recklessness ..." They carried out their duty expertly and that was why Fela received not less than three thousand strokes of *atori* (cane) from both until Fela was seventeen. The effect of that discipline stayed with Fela even at nineteen when he went to England to study. It in fact stayed with him throughout his four and a half years in London and even when he had to holiday compulsorily in Berlin, upon his mother's directives, directly after his studies.

The revolution in song-texts of African rhythms led by Fela has had a lot of side effects. Although many musicians would disclaim any direct influence, yet we are aware that every central force creates off-shoots. The presence of Fela's queens on stage probably had remote influence on the effective emergence of more female singers in Nigeria. We cannot also ignore the contemporary emergence of cultural input now creeping effectively into the song-texts of African Western pop oriented musicians, both male and female. It is not often that "geniuses" like Oliver de Coque, emerge. He claims in his album "Roney, Honey Identity" that he has never been apprenticed to any one in order to understudy making music. He asserted that it was a mysterious gift from God just like we find sweet watery juice naturally trapped inside a coconut pod without knowing how it got inside. By his claim, Oliver de Coque is a leading African guitarists, vocalist, composer, arranger and producer without being a product of any older musician.

Nevertheless, we continue to hear "words of wisdom" from the female voices of Mary Afi Usuah, Joy Nwosu, the Lijadu Sisters, Onyeka Onwenu, Nellie Uchendu, Christy Essien Igbokwe, Theodora Ifudu as well as male pop groups like the Apostles and Tony Grey. It is neither unnatural nor unconventional to conclude with the beginning. Thus, we write the final words with the names of Nigerian Bobby Benson (of Blessed Memory) and Emmanuel Teteh Mensah of Ghana.

Bobby Benson returned to Nigeria in 1947 and died on the 27th of May, 1983. Although E.T Mensah observed that before the advent of highlife, Bobby was playing jazz but he diverted into highlife music and recorded "Taxi Driver." Bobby is unequivocally credited with pioneering highlife in Nigeria. It is important to note that he set in motion the modem rhythm of Nigerian highlife in spite of the fact that E.T. Mensah and Ghana remotely, had to some extent, directly influenced the aesthetics of highlife in Nigeria. Bobby Benson was already dexterous on some of the electronic instruments which he would transfer from jazz to highlife. Bobby Benson Jam Session Orchestra brought in all the early talents who, when jazz declined, went ahead to fashion out jazz highlife. Even the late Rex Lawson whom E.T Mensah credits with taking highlife serious also passed through the "talents developing factory" of Bobby Benson's. Big names, like Victor Olaiya, later to do a joint album with E.T. Mensah as his Nigerian giant-of-highlife-music counterpart, attained maturity under Bobby Benson (including a spell with Samuel Akpabot All Stars Band, Lagos City Orchestra and Ritz Tempo Orchestra) before he "joined hands with the late ABC Cole of West End Coliseum to form the Cool Cats Orchestra" in order to create a distinct sound of his own.

According to Chief Bassey Ita, a young journalist in those days, who were close to Bobby, the great musical "Uncle" accepted he was essentially a jazz-man. In spite of this, Bobby Benson triggered off budding talents who would later become superstars of highlife music. He brought prestige to the vocation by industrializing music and creating the Caban Bamboo as a music floor where tourists had a taste of African dance music culture.

Naturally, when Cassandra left in 1952 and E.T. Mensah had already brought a repertoire of refined highlife music to Nigeria in

1951, Bobby's switch-over to highlife could not be total. In fact, without the merits of the song-text "Taxi Driver", critics and highlife connoisseurs would have paid no attention to Bobby's self conversion from showbiz to dance music. Bobby's primary aim was to introduce and improve live theatre slapstick showbiz but he needed a Cassandra to achieve this goal. Thus, he did not quite see highlife music as an exciting alternative. But E.T. Mensah's tour, with his developed highlife sound and rhythms, including his new indigenous African song-texts, like "Calabar" (done in Nigeria Efik language) was timely. That was why E.T. Mensah meant so much to Nigerian highlife musicians.

Victor Olaiya confirms this: "E.T. Mensah...was an inspiration to me...He in fact dominated highlife scene in Africa in the early fifties. We, the up and coming artists then owe everything to his band, style, arrangement and harmony..." According to Michael Awoyinfa "Olaiya said that although the two of them are giants he would consider himself a shorter giant compared to E.T. Mensah." Olaiya concludes "With his years of experience, his age and discipline, I concede that he is a taller giant."

This study is not as concerned with the sweet rhythms of highlife music which E.T. Mensah introduced as it is with his nationalism and his memorable song-text patriotically produced to mark Ghana's independence anniversary in 1957. Kwasi Aduonum narrates:

> E.T. Mensah was not really a political activist, but he became enthused into the political trade with the influence and inspiration from Dr. Kwame Nkrumah as he preached about "NATIONALISM" in his ideological framework.

Mr. Aduonum continues: "E.T. became engulfed in musical politics as he was invited to perform at the Convention Peoples Party (CPP) rallies at West End Arena. It was this politico-musical interest that he composed Ghana Freedom Highlife in 1957 for the celebration of Ghana's independence." Kwasi Auonum then took a critical look at this nationalistic input by E.T. Mensah and explains that it later became a stumbling block in E.T.'s musical career.

Since E.T. Mensah got into trouble only because he mentioned the names of opposition leaders - Pa Grant, Obetsebi Lamptey and Dr. Danquah, who he considered nationalists in the joint political effort to win independence for Ghana. Kwasi Aduonum's conclusions became relevant:

## Concluding observations

This 'indiscriminate' admixture of political names in the recorded music nearly sent E.T. Mensah to the 'Nsawam' Medium Prisons.

He then summed it all up, "...he went through the offices of Krobo Edusei, Kofi Baako and Dr. Kwame Nkrumah, answering questions about the composition..." As a result of this confrontation, E.T. was either to erase the names of the opposition or C.P.P. members from the record, or an embargo was to be placed on the record. Mr. Kwasi Aduonum then painted a visual verbal picture:

> Gasping for breath and without wasting time E.T. cabled Decca in London to delete the names of Pa Grant, Obetsebi Lamptey and Dr. Danquah from the 10,000 records which were ready for shipment to Ghana.

Probably it is best to look at Robin Mckown's biography of Nkrumah before one draws any meaningful conclusions of the political atmosphere in Ghana at that time. As far as this study is concerned, whatever E.T. Mensah went through, emphasizes the fact that, even as early as the late fifties, song-texts have begun to underline patriotism and nationalism so effectively that the establishment could not underrate its political impact. Dr. Kwame Nkrumah could, in no way, be regarded as a tyrant, given the political arm-twisting in Ghana then, which led to his imprisonment. He won the elections for Ghana's self-rule when he was behind bars. It was an exciting bravery to convert directly from prison to Government house; and from the status of a prisoner to that of Ghana's first Prime Minister. Thus, E.T. went ahead to compose the "Nigerian Freedom Highlife" for the celebration of Nigeria's independence in 1960. He also created a historical document which publicized regional political unions in Africa, based on Nkrumah's experiment, which aimed at breaking the political walls erected with the phrases "Anglo" and "Franco". That song, recorded by E.T. Mensah, was captioned "Ghana-Guinea-Mali" highlife whose song-text was written by Joe Eyeson.

To really confirm his Pan Africanist role, his tours also covered Cote d' Voire, Senegal, Liberia, Guinea and Sierra Leone. To project highlife externally, E. T. Mensah toured England.

From Nigeria, Victor Olaiya, by his coverage of Queen Elizabeth the Second's tour of Nigeria, showed the same urge to build an image for Africa as early as 1956. By adapting highlife to compete in a

European jazz festival, he already projected the elastic nature of highlife, pointing towards its growth. His song-texts also functioned as national unification tools. He composed songs in Igbo, Efik, Hausa and his own native Yoruba language in order to communicate more effectively.

Song-texts of African urban popular music rhythm could be entertaining but they are functionally the voice of the community. They are equally the conscience of African societies, it is through these lyrics that African domestic and external politics can be monitored. Song-texts act as the thermometer for measuring African political, social and economic temperature. Sex and love are never publicized, they are treated with reverence; and they are also regarded as trivial and incompatible with the serious problems of Africa.

You may talk about protest and freedom charts in apartheid South Africa or pre-independence colonial era in most African countries, but within independent African nations, song-texts discuss neo-colonialism, cultural piracy, inflation, austerity, indiscipline, politics, domestic issues and whatever was current on the political, cultural, economic and social table of the nation. The style and approach depends on the artist. Song-texts could be directly confrontational, militant, propaganda-oriented, satirical, gospelic or narrative. Whatever may be the form, the themes revolve around poverty, apartheid or neo-colonialism (domestic or external) and invocations to God as the ultimate hope when all else fails. Because the "language of music" is universal, a foreigner may be moved by the rhythm of African urban popular music to dance when the floor is exclusively thrown open to the deaf-and-dumb.

There is need for highlife music countries of West Africa to hold symposia for "standardizing" highlife music in order to universalize it as a dance rhythm which could be read and played even by Western musicologists and musicians.

# Appendix

## Lyrics and corresponding musical scores

It is functional, in the context of this work to have the lyrics as the focus on the musician's messages. Lyrics as the town-crier's communal and communicating package would be uniquely highlighted and delivered as a "mass media" anchor.

A number of musicians spread across Nigeria, unaware that this work was motivated by my desire to monumentalize their contributions, towards the growth of highlife music; and its offspring refused to make themselves available to me and my field assistants, for a chat.

The limitation of this work, to a mere foundation level, is to a great extent, caused by such short vision, unmindful of the impact this work will make academically and professionally. Indeed this Appendix houses a meager sample of what I referred to on the original draft as nightclub rhetorics (or communal messages) designed to effect social, political and economic changes in the society.

The fact that whenever a musician's masterpiece fades, he drops off the public's mental limelight or of his consumer's and patron's; concerns me deeply. There had to be a way of erecting monuments about him to replace the ephemeral evaluation, characteristic of the consumer-ship, by his clientele. Is this one of the ways?

## Okukuseku Success Band of Ghana

>    Money no dey
>    Pocket no good (pidgin)
>    Na waah - o
>    Money no dey
>    Pocket no good
>    Na so so suffer suffer
>    Na waah - o

Money no dey
Pocket no good

III
Everyday, I dey work, work
But I no dey see money-
My brother I dey tire
Na waah.

Pocket no good
1 dey find money
But I no dey see money
Na waah-o.

Today, you go see me for Lagos
Tomorrow, I dey for Benin-City
I dey go Onitsha
After that you go see me for Enugu.

Na wetin dey happen?
Sebi, I dey find money
I dey go to Aba
I dey go to Warri
I dey go to Port Harcourt
And then to Kano
And wetin dey worry me?
Money palaver
Na waah-o!

I sabi some people
Them no dey work
But them get plenty money
Na me dey work
Ne me dey suffer
Na me dey tire
But I no dey get money.

Na Waah
1 dey pray to God
Mek e help me
Mek I get money
The day I go get money
I do not know
Better thank
I go give my God
My brother,
I dey tire

Na waah
My brother, I dey tire
My brother, I dey suffer
My brother, I dey tire
My brother, I dey suffer

## Okukuseku Success Band of Ghana

### *Who Sabi Tomorrow? (Pidgin)*

Who sabi?
Who sabi tomorrow? Who sabi?
You say you so know
Mind your own business
Mind your own business
You say you so know
Mind your own business
My brother
Mind your own business
Your own business na your own

Somebody don get him own business
You don't know how manage e get-am
Somebody don marry wife
Don't know how manage e marry-am
But always you are making con - concern
But always you are making Arithmetic on it
Mister, you say you so know
This business na me get-am
So. no make con-concern for me
I beg you
Leave me alone
Mek I do my own
No put sand sand in my own
Na God give me
Na God dash me

Somebody don build him house
You don't know how manage e build-am
Somebody get him own business
You don't know how manage manage e get-am
Always you are making kankama
But always you are making wayo.

Mister, you say you so know
This business name get-am
So. no make con-concern for me.

# Index

Achibong -71
Adolf Doku -4
African brothers -46, 47
African music Research Party -4
African Pyramids Band -6, 142
African Rhythm & African Sensibility -30
Afrobeat -3, 6, 9, 10
Atua Agyepong -48
Agu Norris -58, 60, 141
Ajilo hair-do -4, 62
Akompi Guitar Band -7
Akwasi Sampong -44
Alade music show -61
All African Festival of Arts -83
All Stars Band -4, 66, 81, 153
Amos Tutuola -152
Ampadu Boateng-38, 46
Anambra Broadcasting Corporation - 98, 145
Andy Man International Band -108
Angus Okolie -22, 23, 24
Appiah Agykum Band -35
Arinze E. C. -8, 21, 56, 58, 81, 152, 153
Art Alade -51, 61, 65
*Artists* -88, 96

Awila -108
Baby Face Paul -4, 70, 72
Balla Miller -4, 6, 50, 52, 63, 142, 144, 151, 153
Balladism -20
Bassy Ita -158
British Broadcasting Corporation -89, 124, 130
Bens-Ajilo -67
Biafran Soldiers -99, 118
Biafran War -13
Biddy Uchendu -114
Bill Friday -4, 43, 60, 66, 145
Black Beat Band -7
Bob Cole -48
Bob Hughes -4
Bob Marley -10, 11, 12, 25, 151
Bobby Benson -3, 4, 12, 16, 50, 52, 55, 58, 59, 66, 67, 68, 69, 70, 128, 141, 146, 148, 150, 157, 158
Bobby Cassandra -4, 69, 158
Bobby Jam Session Orchestra -70
Bola Johnson -142
Bongos Ikwue -24, 51, 102, 128, 142, 145
Braimah J.K -34
British Pateralism -4

Broadcasting Corporation of Nigeria -91
Broadcasting Corporation of Northern Nigeria -91
Broadway Dance Band -7, 132, 133
Brook Benton -106
Brothers Emmanuel & Lazarus -3
C.K Mann -41, 42, 43, 47, 48
    - king of highlife -43
Calabar Brass Band -65
Calypso -26
Carlos Moore -30, 31, 33, 34
Carousel 7 -42, 48
Celestine Obiakor -54, 98
Celestine Ukwu -25, 56, 107, 109, 113, 114, 140, 148
    -and his Philosophies Band -113
Charlie Uwuege -99
Charlotte Dada -48
Chernoff -56
Chinua Achebe -151
Chris Ajilo -4, 61, 66, 145, 146
    -and his Cubanos -62
    -hair do-62
Chris Nwaiga -141
Chris Odiase -59
Chris Okotie -21, 152
    -fan club -152
Christy Essien -157
Chuks Nwamana -145
Cliff Richards -81
Codiac -19
Cool Cats Band -63, 67, 158
Cornie Ajilo -66
Country Modinaires -81
Dairo I..K. -16, 71, 142
Dan Chie Awere -39
Dan Maraya -71, 72, 88, 89
    -and his kuntigi -88, 89, 90
Dan Satch Ayo -108, 109, 140, 145, 148
Dayspring Dance Band -132
Decca West Africa -17, 19, 38, 39, 57, 60, 108

Dizzy Aquaye -81
Dollar Nite -29
Dolly Parton -15
Don Williams -21
Dr. Sir Warrior -107, 108, 121
Dustus Springfield -117
E.K. Band -7, 38, 39
E.K. Nyame -38, 45
Eastern New Time Orchestra -69
Easy Life Top Beats -142
Ebenezer (Obey) Olasupo Fabiyi -2, 26, 43, 71, 120, 152
Ebun Clark -5
Eddie Okonta -4, 59, 72, 81, 144
Eddie Okwedi -145
Eddie Roberts -13
Eddyson -67
Efik cultural music -71
*Ekassa* -77
*Ekombo* -3
Elvis Presley -81
EMI -85, 86, 126, 127, 144,
Empire Rhythm Orchestra -8, 56, 57, 58, 59, 60
Etim Udoh - 81
Etubon Rex Williams -122
Ezewuiro Chris Obinna -111
Fedinand Chams -112
Fela Anikulapo Kuti -2, 3, 6, 8, 9, 20, 21, 25, 28, 29, 30, 31, 32, 33, 34, 35, 52, 54, 56, 57, 130, 141, 151, 152, 154, 155, 156, 157
    -biography -33
    -brother -67
    -father -51, 156
    -generation tree -33
    -messiah-ship -33
    -mother -51, 156
    -wives -33
Fela Sowande -62
Felix Liberty -21
Festac '77 -62, 83, 92, 118
First World Negro Festival – 142
Folk music -96
Folklore -97

Frank Hayfron -39, 40
Fuji – 150
Gbenga Ayodele -31, 32
Ghanaian
   -highlife band -44
   -highlife in -48
   -highlife language -45
   -music -44, 95
   -musician -37, 44
   -vocalists -6
God -101
Godwin Omabuwa -21
Grand Order of the Havana -9, 83
Great Orientals -108
Green Vergineers -113
Groovies -106
Guitar Playtime -93
Guy Warren -4
Gyasi G.K -37, 47
   -and noble kings -37, 41
Harold Courlander -51
Harriman and his colleagues -3
Harry Mosco -113
Havana Carnival Nite -8, 29, 36, 58, 60
Havana Nite Club -145
Headlines -22
Herbert Udemba -54, 100
   -and his Africali -101
   -West Africa Babies Party -101
Highlife music -1, 2, 3, 4, 5, 68, 149, 151
   -ballad -52
   -dance band -4
   -emerged from -37
   -Ghanaian -7
   -growth of -4
   -history of- 15
   -in Ghana -44, 48
   -institutional vectors -15
   -jazz -52
   -king of -146
   -modern -71
   -musicians -52
   -Nigeria -7
   -origin -37
   -ozidi -52
   -song-texts-1
   -use of Hausa in -6
Hilltop Singers -117
Homzy Continental International -119
Hot Shots -59
Hubert Ogunde -4, 20, 69, 74, 75
Hykker's International -13, 14
Ichika -108
Ify Jerry -13
Ikenga Superstars -6
Instrument -44, 48
International Performing Rights Society -70
Inyang Henshaw -3, 4, 6, 25, 52, 68, 132, 133, 143, 144
Inyang Obot -66
Israel Nwoba-6, 20, 21, 22, 23, 24, 25, 26, 35, 54, 71, 100, 142
Jake Solo -13, 141
Jam Session Orchestra -69, 70
James Brown -11
Jazz -3
Jerry Hansen -34, 40, 47
   -and the Ramblers Dance Band -39
Jide Obi -21, 114
Jim Christian -67
Jim Reeves -21, 77
Jimmy Cliff -10, 14, 145
Joe Kelly -4
Joe Mensah -43, 45
Joe Nez -72, 107
Jofabro -81
John Chukwu -28, 29
John Ikediani -108
John Miller Chernoff -30
Johnny Nash -30
Joromy Recording and Television Studio -83
Joy Nwosu -157
Justline Akwata -113

Kabaka -108
Kabaka International Band -108
Kakaiku Guitar Band -42, 47
Kalakuta Republic -115
   -Republic Sack -156
Kenny Rogers -106
King Kennytone and his Western Top Toppers -143
Kings College -80
Kingsley Bassy -70
Kobina Okai- 38, 45
Kofi Yankwon -43
Koola Lobitos -29, 34
Kwasi Aduonum -34, 159
Kwasi Ampadu-Boateng -35, 36
Kwesi Plange -39
Lagos City Orchestra -158
Laz Ekweme -119
Lidaju Sisters -157
Lord Kitchener's Calypso -21
Mambo dance -59
Mamman Shaffa -71, 72
Marcus Garvey -10, 15
Mary Afi Usua -120, 157
Melody Maestros -81
Melvin Okachi -13, 83
Member of the Order of the Niger -9, 83, 92
Mensah -4, 5, 7, 16, 36, 37, 39, 51, 58, 60, 64, 68, 70, 81, 122, 123, 148, 150, 151, 157, 158, 159, 160
   -and Ghana's repertory-36
   -king of highlife -36
Mighty Sparrow -10, 21
Mike Falana -67
Mike Ejeagha -52, 93,113
Mike Enahoro -13, 50, 54, 55, 56
Mike Obianuwu -113, 118, 119
Miriam Makeba -120
Mono Mono -13, 83, 84, 85, 141
Moonlight Professionals -70
*Morning Post* -142
Music -72, 87, 124
   -African -63
   -teachers of -63

Musicians -16, 53, 72, 76, 81, 88, 93, 96, 114, 120, 128, 154
   -female -120
   -modern -77
   -Nigerian -50, 53, 129, 130
   -Union -75
National Council of Nigeria and the Cameroons -74
Native Authority Police Band -100
Nelly Uchendu -113, 114, 142, 157
Nelson Mandela -28
Nicholas Mgbarga -53, 54, 56, 124, 127, 152
Nigeria -87
Nigeria Armed Forces -155
Nigeria Broadcasting Service -61, 91, 93, 153
Nigeria Civil War -13, 57, 99, 116, 146, 147, 148
Nigeria Institute of Music -61
Nigeria Police Band -131
Nigeria Sound Makers Band -75
Nigerian Civil War -92
Nigerphone -18
Nketia H.N - 44, 152
Ocean Strings -42
*Ofege* -3, 13, 83, 84, 86
Ogbanje -135, 136, 145, 146, 147
Ogunde Theatre Party -4
Okonkwo Adigwe -72
Ola Balogun -28
Oliver de Coque -56, 157
Onyeka Owenu -12, 25, 150
Onyekwelu's C.T Niger Phone -18, 19, 93, 100
Onyina Guitar Band -7
Order of the British Empire -17
Oriental Brothers International Band -3
Osagyefo, Nkrumah Kwame -15, 45
Osibi -37
Osita Osadebe -2, 3, 6, 25, 56, 72, 78, 126
Oyelima highlife -2, 6
Ozzidism -25, 26, 27, 35

# Index

P MAN– 18, 88, 111
   -chairman -77
Pan Africanism -10, 25, 30
Pan Africanists -2, 10, 20, 26, 125
Paperback Limited -27
Pat Fin -13
Pat Thomas -42
Patsol -27, 70, 72, 143
Patty Obassey -133, 148
Paulson Kalu -77
Peter Tosh -10, 14, 25, 26
Phillips West Africa Records -17, 27, 57, 70, 81, 82, 140, 142, 143, 144, 147
Pick Ups -57, 81
Piracy -19
Police Band -132
Polygram RecordingCompany -18, 19, 61, 78, 86, 145
Professional Seagulls -145
Queen Elizabeth II -17, 45, 64, 132, 133, 150, 160
Quincy Jones -15
Railway Silver Band -7
Ralph Adusah -41
Rambles International Band -7, 8, 9
Recording Company -16, 71
Red Sports Band -7
Reggae -26
Rendevous Dance Band -131, 133
Rendezvous Dandres Orchestra -68
Rex Lawson -4, 6, 7, 9, 56, 64, 72, 82, 111, 132, 140, 143, 147, 151, 152, 158
   -and his Rivermen – 146
Rex Williams -4, 123
Rhythm Stars -98
Rhythms -27
Ritz Tempo Orchestra -158
Rogers All Star -19, 127, 128
Ron Kwofie -4, 5
Roy Chicago -4, 55, 141, 146
Sahara All Stars -68
Saka Acquaye -4

Sam Cook -106, 107
Sammy Akpabot -4, 50, 66, 131, 132, 133, 144, 153, 158
   -all stars-158
Sammy Lartey -51, 66
Sammy Obot -131, 132, 133, 146
Saturday in Lagos -143
Segun Buknor -80
Sensational Comrade Rock Band – 112
Shawna Moore -30, 33
Sifo Lawson -66
Sigma Club of Ibadan University -7, 8, 9, 29, 36, 58, 60, 83, 140, 143
Sir Warrior and his Oriental International Band -108
Song-text – 21, 27, 154, 160
   -revolution in -157
   -20-Swahili & Zulus-21
Sonny Okosun -3, 12, 19, 25, 26, 28, 26, 35, 56, 110, 120, 129, 141, 144
Sonny Oti -98, 114, 119, 133
*Spear* -32
St. Gregory College Boys -13, 54, 81, 83, 84, 85
Stan Plange -51
Stargazers Dance Band -7
Stephen Amechi -59, 60, 68, 73, 74, 98, 99
Steve Rhodes -57, 58, 59, 153
Style -106
Sunny Ade -26, 71, 120, 152
Sweet Breeze -113
Tabansi -19, 92, 141
*Tales of Yoruba gods & heroes -51*
Tempos Band of Ghana -4, 45, 60, 77, 81, 41
The Abibifo Band -41
The Afro Beats -41
The Ambassador -41
The Apostles -13
The black race -41
The boys -16, 17
The Complex Sounds -41
The Comrades Rock Band -113

*The Daily News* -34
The girls -17
The Harbours -68
The Old Masters -89
The Postmen -27
The Republicans -7
The Spangle -118
The Strangers -13
The Sweet breeze -13
The Wavelength -113
The Wings -13
Theodora Ifudu -14, 157
*Three Nights Wizards* -6, 20
Tom Davies -106
Tommy Obeyi -98, 99
Tony Grey -14, 157
*Top life* -54, 55
Top Ten Aces -69
Toppest -106
Tunde King -64
TV & Radio houses -112, 113, 130

Uhuru Dance Band -7, 132, 133, 146
Unibello Brothers -104
Universal Hotel Band -67
Victor Olaiya -4, 6, 36, 55, 59, 64, 66, 67, 70, 81, 123, 132, 133, 146, 150, 151, 153, 158, 160
Victor Uwaifo -3, 6, 8, 9, 13, 27, 29, 51, 52, 54, 56, 57, 78, 123, 144, 151
   -family of -79, 84
   -Sir -82
White Star Musical Party -43, 71
William Du Bois -10
William Onyeabo -114
Willie -35
Willie Payne -58, 59
Wilrim -19
Wole Soyinka – 152
Zeal Onyia -4, 21, 51, 55, 67, 70, 74, 118, 119, 142, 144

www.ingramcontent.com/pod-product-compliance
Lightning Source LLC
Chambersburg PA
CBHW021125300426
44113CB00006B/291